THE
FOUNDERS

THE
FOUNDERS

*The 39 Stories Behind
the U.S. Constitution*

DENNIS BRINDELL FRADIN

ILLUSTRATIONS BY
MICHAEL McCURDY

Walker & Company
NEW YORK

For April Ann Fradin, Michael James Richard, and
Rebecca Batey Fradin, with love —D. B. F.

To the O'Sullivan family,
especially Maureen O'Sullivan —M. M.

Text copyright © 2005 by Dennis Brindell Fradin
Illustrations copyright © 2005 by Michael McCurdy

First published in the United States of America in 2005 by Walker Publishing Company, Inc.

Distributed to the trade by Holtzbrinck Publishers

For information about permission to reproduce selections from this book, write to Permissions,
Walker & Company, 104 Fifth Avenue, New York, New York 10011

Library of Congress Cataloging-in-Publication Data
available upon request
ISBN 0-8027-8972-2 (hardcover)
ISBN-13 978-0-8027-8972-3 (hardcover)
ISBN 0-8027-8973-0 (reinforced)
ISBN-13 978-0-8027-8973-0 (reinforced)

The illustrations in this book were created on scratchboard.

Book design by Claire Counihan
Book composition by Coghill Composition Company

Visit Walker & Company's Web site at www.walkeryoungreaders.com

Printed in the United States of America

2 4 6 8 10 9 7 5 3 1

CONTENTS

INTRODUCTION

Today we spell the name of our country *United States*, with a capital *U* and a capital *S*. This was not the case in the nation's first years. Atop the Declaration of Independence, which announced the country's birth, it read:

IN CONGRESS, JULY 4, 1776.
THE UNANIMOUS DECLARATION OF THE THIRTEEN
UNITED STATES OF AMERICA

Sometimes *both* words—*united states*—went uncapitalized. For example, on March 1, 1781, the young country placed a national framework of government into effect. Called the Articles of Confederation, it repeatedly referred to the nation as "the united states," with a small *u* and a small *s*. Likewise, when Americans of the 1770s and the 1780s wrote letters or newspaper articles, they usually wrote the country's name "united states" or "united States."

On the other hand, when writing about individual states, Americans of that era almost always used a capital *S*, such as the "State of Pennsylvania," the "State of South Carolina," or the "State of Virginia."

There was a reason that the new country's citizens capitalized "States" when referring to individual states but wrote "united states" or "united States" when referring to the entire nation. A majority of Americans didn't think the country's name was a proper noun. In fact, they didn't exactly think of the United States as being a country. Although all thirteen states had worked together to break free of Britain, most Americans viewed this as a temporary necessity to win the Revolution and considered their states more important than the nation as a whole. Americans also feared that a strong federal government would tax them relentlessly and exert too much control over their lives. The Articles of Confederation pleased most Americans by creating a weak central government, saying that the "united states" was merely a "league of friendship" between the "States."

The federal government was nearly helpless in many ways during the country's early years. The entire united states army consisted of only several hundred men and was so weak that it could not defend the country if trouble arose. There was no president as we know the nation's chief executive today, but only a president of the Continental Congress who had little power or influence. There were no federal courts to settle cases of national importance. There was no national currency, so states printed their own money, which had different values from state to state.

The national government lacked the authority to collect taxes. When money was needed, Congress could only beg the thirteen states for it. The states often ignored these requests, with the result that in a typical year Congress might ask for $8,000,000 and receive only about $400,000. The bottom line was that Congress could not pay all its debts.

Because each state was in many ways stronger than the federal government, the best lawmakers often chose to serve in local government rather than in the Continental Congress. Perhaps Gouverneur Morris of Pennsylvania was exaggerating when he called the national congressmen "a lot of rascals," but in many cases they were what we might call the B team among politicians.

To make things worse, the united states had no permanent capital. Philadelphia, Pennsylvania, had been the national capital when the Declaration of Independence had been adopted in 1776. But over the next several years the capital was moved *nine* times. Cities and towns that served as the national capital between late 1776 and 1787 were Baltimore, Maryland; Philadelphia, Pennsylvania; Lancaster, Pennsylvania (one day); York, Pennsylvania; Philadelphia again; Princeton, New Jersey; Annapolis, Maryland; Trenton, New Jersey; and New York City.

Several events demonstrated that the federal government needed to be strengthened. For example, in June 1783 about one hundred soldiers who were owed their back pay by the u.s. government surrounded Independence Hall in Philadelphia, where Congress was meeting. The soldiers broke windows and shouted that they wanted their money. Lacking the funds, the congressmen packed their bags and ran away to Princeton, New Jersey, which became the national capital for the next four months.

Shays's Rebellion also revealed the inadequacy of the national government. In this revolt, which lasted from the fall of 1786 until early 1787, Massachusetts farmers led by Daniel Shays and others demanded lower taxes and an end to the imprisonment of debtors. Since the federal government didn't have a big enough army to end the revolt, the Massachusetts state militia had to do it.

When he heard about Shays's Rebellion, George Washington feared that the entire nation would collapse. "Without some alteration in our political creed," Washington wrote to his friend James Madison in the fall of 1786, "the superstructure we have been seven years raising at the expense of so much blood and treasure, must fall. We are fast verging to anarchy and confusion!"

By then, most Americans agreed with the man who had led the nation to victory in the Revolutionary War. In September 1786 a meeting was held in Annapolis, Maryland, to discuss possible changes in the Articles of Confederation. All thirteen states were invited, but only Delaware, New Jersey, New York, Pennsylvania, and Virginia sent delegates to this conference. Despite not achieving much, the Annapolis Convention issued a call for a much larger meeting to be held in Philadelphia. On February 21, 1787, the Continental Congress issued its own call for a convention to strengthen the federal government.

Fearful of being swallowed up by a more powerful central government, Rhode Island, the smallest of the thirteen states, sent no delegates to the convention that opened in Philadelphia's Independence Hall on May 25, 1787. The other twelve states sent a total of fifty-five delegates who in many cases came and went during the four-month-long proceedings. On the opening day, George Washington was unanimously elected convention president.

At the start, many of the delegates expected to merely improve the Articles of Confederation. But to amend the articles, every state had to approve the changes. The chances were slim that all thirteen states could agree on *anything*, and besides, Rhode Island wasn't even there to present its views. The delegates decided to scrap the articles and produce a new national framework of government, which became known as the United States Constitution.

It was also decided that, as a matter of procedure, each state delegation would have a single vote on every issue proposed at the convention. For example, if a state had five delegates at the convention, three would have to vote yes for that state's vote to be registered in favor of a particular issue. A simple majority of states had to vote yes for a proposal to be incorporated into the Constitution.

For four months, the delegates worked nearly every day, Monday through Saturday, generally from early in the morning until about 4:00 p.m. They soon agreed on the basics. The new government would have three branches: legislative, executive, and judicial. But they disagreed, often bitterly, on the details. Would the legislative branch have one house or two, and what would determine how many legislators each state would have? How would the president, or head of the executive branch, be chosen, and how long would the president serve? What if the judicial branch, or federal courts, had a conflict with local courts in the various states?

At times the arguing became so heated that it appeared the convention would disband without creating a constitution. On those occasions, Ben Franklin or someone else would patch things up with an amusing story or a few conciliatory words. Gradually, the delegates realized that the best way to get anything done was to compromise. For example, there were suggestions that the president serve a fifteen-, eleven-, eight-, seven-, four-, or three-year term. Some wanted the president to be eligible for reelection. Some didn't. There was even a suggestion that the nation have not one but *three* presidents. It was finally agreed that the nation would have a single president who could be reelected to any number of four-year terms.

The fiercest clashes were between the "large" (more populous) and the "small" (less populous) states. At that time the largest states were Virginia, Pennsylvania, North Carolina, and Massachusetts, in order of population. Expecting to one day be crowded with people, South Carolina and Georgia often sided with the large states. The smaller states were New York, which was not yet the population giant it later became, Maryland, Connecticut, New Jersey, New Hampshire, and Delaware. Rhode Island was a small state, too, but wanted no part of the proceedings.

James Madison, who became known as the Father of the Constitution because of his many contributions to the document, was the chief architect of the Virginia Plan, also called the Large-State Plan. It proposed a two-house legislature: the House of Representatives and the Senate. The membership of both houses would be proportional to population, meaning the more people a state had, the more senators and representatives it would be entitled to.

The small-state delegates reacted with anger. If representation were based strictly on population, they pointed out, the small states would have virtually no power in Congress. They countered with the New Jersey Plan, also called the Small-State Plan. It proposed a one-house legislature in which each state would have a single vote.

Now it was the large-state delegates who howled in protest. Why should the small states have as much say in the legislature as the most populous states? At times the dispute over this issue became so heated that it appeared the delegates might give up and go home. Roger Sherman of Connecticut saved the day by proposing a compromise: a state's population would determine its membership in the House of Representatives, but each state would be equally represented in the Senate. This Connecticut Compromise, as it is called, was adopted. That is why each state has two U.S. senators but anywhere from just one to several dozen members of the House of Representatives.

Another topic of dispute was slavery, which was dying out in the North but growing in the South. Should the Constitution ban the continued importation of slaves into the country?

Yes, said many northern delegates. No, said most southerners. Again, a compromise was reached. It was agreed that Congress could prohibit the importation of slaves, but not until 1808. This was actually a triumph for the South, for by then the country would have so many slaves that the evil institution could continue without bringing in any new ones.

Since population would determine a state's membership in the House of Representatives, how should slaves be counted? As people, insisted the southerners. That wasn't fair, said the northerners. Slaves were treated as property, so why should they suddenly be counted as people just so that southern states could have more representatives? Once more each side gave way a little, resulting in the oddest compromise in the Constitution. For the sake of determining membership in the House, each slave was to be counted as three-fifths of a person.

Point by point, the delegates worked out the details of the Constitution. New states could join the country, they decided, but no new state could be carved from an existing state without its consent. In case of conflict between a federal and a state law, the federal law was to be "the supreme law of the land." If they wanted to alter or add to the Constitution, Americans could amend it with the approval of three-fourths of the states.

When they finished hammering out the articles of the Constitution, the delegates turned them over to the five-man Committee on Style to create a coherent document. Pennsylvanian Gouverneur Morris of this committee did most of the actual writing of the Constitution. As a result, the wording of the great document is largely his handiwork.

On the last day of the convention—September 17, 1787—the Constitution was signed. Thirteen of the fifty-five delegates had left early, either because they opposed the Constitution or because they needed to attend to personal or public business. The thirteen delegates who left before signing the document were Caleb Strong of Massachusetts; Oliver Ellsworth of Connecticut; John Lansing and Robert Yates of New York; William Churchill Houston of New Jersey; Luther Martin and John Francis Mercer of Maryland; James McClurg and George Wythe of Virginia; William Richardson Davie and Alexander Martin of North Carolina; and William Houstoun and William Pierce of Georgia. Three delegates who were present at the end objected to the Constitution so strenuously that they refused to sign: Elbridge Gerry of Massachusetts and George Mason and Edmund Randolph of Virginia.

The remaining thirty-nine men signed the Constitution. They are called the Founding Fathers, or simply the founders (although some people also place the sixteen nonsigners in this category).

According to Article VII of the Constitution, the document would take effect if nine states ratified or approved it. Despite having called themselves states since 1776, the thirteen former colonies wouldn't become states in the modern sense until they ratified the Constitution. The states began to schedule their own conventions of leaders to consider the new framework of government. Some states had about as many opponents of the Constitution (called Anti-Federalists) as supporters (called Federalists), so it was not certain whether the document would be approved by the required nine states.

Delaware, at its convention in Dover, became the first state to approve the Constitution, on Friday, December 7, 1787. Delaware has been called the First State ever since. Pennsylvania went second, ratifying the Constitution five days later, on December 12. New Jersey became state number three six days after that, on December 18, 1787.

The new year brought good news for the Federalists, with Georgia becoming the fourth state on January 2, 1788. A week later on January 9 a convention in Hartford approved the Constitution, making Connecticut the fifth state.

The outlook for the Federalists appeared bleak in Massachusetts, where a convention to consider the Constitution opened in Boston the day of Connecticut's ratification. Massachusetts's vote was crucial, for it would influence other states and could mean ultimate victory or defeat for the Constitution. When the convention opened, slightly more than half the delegates were Anti-Federalists. The Antis included two of Massachusetts's greatest leaders, Samuel Adams and John Hancock, but Paul Revere helped change that.

Paul Revere knew that his friend Samuel Adams had the utmost respect for working people's opinions. One day Revere informed Adams that so many Boston workingmen had come to the Green Dragon Tavern to show approval for the Constitution that they had spilled out into the streets. When Adams asked how many were in the streets, Revere answered, "More than there are stars in the sky."

The workingmen's support changed Samuel Adams's mind, and a similar visit by some Federalists helped change Hancock's. Adams and Hancock spoke in favor of the Constitution at the Massachusetts convention. As a result, the Bay State approved the Constitution on February 6, 1788, by a vote of 187 in favor to 168 opposed.

On April 28, 1788, nearly three months after Massachusetts became the sixth state, Maryland became the seventh. A month later, on May 23, South Carolina became the eighth state to ratify the Constitution. Now only a single additional state was needed for the Constitution to go into effect.

In mid-1788, New Hampshire leaders met at Concord to consider the Constitution. On June 21, 1788, by a slim margin of 57 to 47, the convention voted to adopt the new governmental framework. With this vote New Hampshire became the ninth state and the Constitution became the law of the land for a strengthened nation: the United States of America.

But now Americans faced a new dilemma. What about the four states that hadn't approved the Constitution? By not accepting the new federal framework, Virginia, New York, North Carolina, and Rhode Island were almost like separate foreign countries outside the United States.

Virginia's convention turned into a terrific battle. James Madison, known as the Father of the Constitution, argued for its adoption. James Monroe, who like Madison would one day become president of the United States, was among the Antis. The Federalists won by a close 89–79 vote on June 25, 1788, and Virginia became state number ten.

New York also had a fierce struggle. In fact, the Antis might have won there were it not for Alexander Hamilton's efforts on behalf of the Constitution. As it was, the New York convention voted its approval by the razor-thin margin of 30 in favor and 27 opposed. That day—July 26, 1788—New York became our eleventh state.

The Constitution didn't protect basic rights of citizens, many Antis complained. This was a reason why North Carolina and Rhode Island withheld their approval. Thanks largely to James Madison, the process of adding what proved to be the first ten amendments to the Constitution was under way by 1789. Called the Bill of Rights, these amendments, which protect freedom of speech, the right to a fair trial, and other basic rights, weren't approved until late 1791. However, the fact that they were being created helped persuade North Carolina to become our twelfth state by approving the Constitution on November 21, 1789.

What about Rhode Island, the smallest state and the only one not to have sent any delegates to the Constitutional Convention? Was Rhode Island to be a little country of its own in the midst of the United States? Rhode Islanders argued among themselves, with the city of Providence even threatening to withdraw from Rhode Island and join the United States under its Constitution by itself. That didn't happen, and finally, at a convention in Newport, Rhode Island approved the Constitution by a vote of 34 in favor to 32 opposed on May 29, 1790.

This breathtakingly close vote made Rhode Island the thirteenth state and meant that the framework of government signed by the thirty-nine founders was in effect throughout the country, as it has been ever since.

Note: In the following chapters the states are presented in the order in which they approved the Constitution, not the sequence in which they signed the document. Also, within each state, the founders aren't presented in the order in which they signed but in a way that tells the story of the Constitution. In Virginia, for example, James Madison is placed ahead of George Washington because Madison was the Father of the Constitution and Washington then became the first president under the Constitution.

I. DELAWARE

In 1638 Sweden became the first European country to begin permanent colonization of Delaware. During Swedish rule, America's first log cabins were built in Delaware. The Dutch (the people of the Netherlands) took control of Delaware in 1655 before England seized the region in 1664. The English named Delaware for Lord De La Warr, a governor of Virginia.

It was said that, in the Revolutionary era, the new U.S. flag was flown for the first time in Delaware. Reportedly this occurred on September 3, 1777, at the Battle of Cooch's Bridge. That year Dover became Delaware's state capital, as it still is today.

By 1787, Delaware was the least populous of the thirteen states. Most of Delaware's fifty-five thousand people lived on small farms, where they grew corn and wheat and raised chickens, cows, and pigs.

At the Constitutional Convention, Delaware's delegates fought for the rights of the small states. Rather than form a government dominated by the large states, one of them advised, the country should eliminate states totally! Another threatened that Delaware might withdraw from the country rather than be pushed around by the large states.

Delaware's leaders were pleased with the finished product. On December 7, 1787, less than three months after the convention ended, Delaware ratified the Constitution before any other state, earning the nickname the First State.

DELAWARE

Name	Birth Date	Age at Signing	Marriage(s)	Children	Death Date	Age at Death
JOHN DICKINSON	November 8, 1732	54	Polly Norris	5	February 14, 1808	75
GEORGE READ*	September 18, 1733	53	Gertrude Ross Till	5	September 21, 1798	65
GUNNING BEDFORD JR.	1747	About 40	Jane Ballereau Parker	5	March 30, 1812	About 65
JACOB BROOM	1752	About 35	Rachel Pierce	8	April 25, 1810	About 58
RICHARD BASSETT	April 2, 1745	42	Ann Ennals Betsy Garnett	2	August 16, 1815, or September 15, 1815	70

Note: "Children" refers to the total number of children each founder was known to have fathered by his wife (or wives if married more than once).

An asterisk (*) after a founder's name indicates that he also signed the Declaration of Independence.

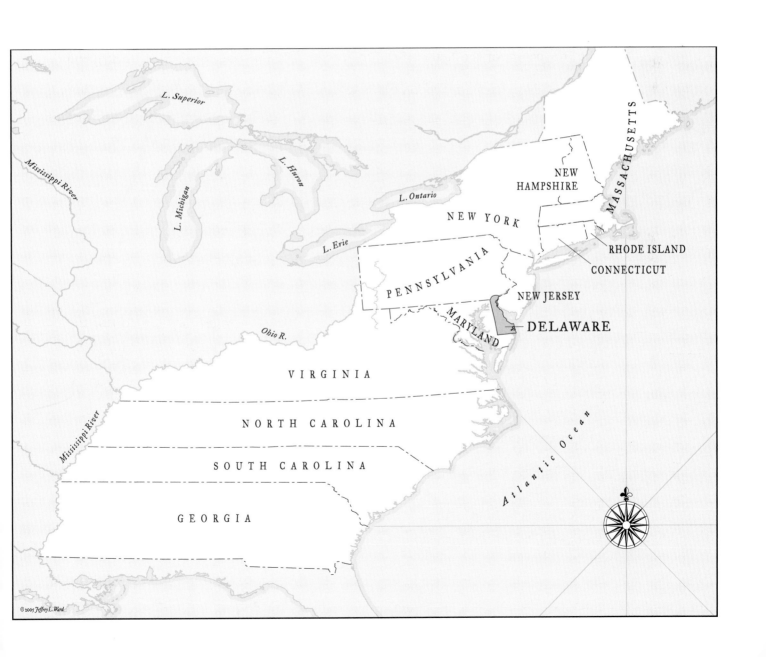

JOHN DICKINSON
"The Power of the People"

John Dickinson

JOHN DICKINSON WAS BORN into a wealthy Quaker family in Maryland's Talbot County on November 8, 1732. At the age of eight, John moved into a mansion near Dover, Delaware. He received much of his early education from William Killen, a tutor from Ireland who later became Delaware's chief justice. Young John did have one odd study habit. Believing it was healthier, he read standing up rather than sitting in a chair.

To prepare for a law career, John went to work for Philadelphia attorney John Moland in 1750. He and another of Moland's law students, George Read, became close friends. At twenty-one, Dickinson sailed to England, where he studied law in London for about three years. In 1757 he returned to America, where he practiced law in both Pennsylvania and Delaware.

Dickinson discovered, however, that politics interested him more than law. He served in the Delaware colonial legislature from 1760 to 1762 and in the Pennsylvania Colony's legislature from 1762 to 1765. In 1770 he married a Philadelphia woman, Mary Norris, known as Polly. The couple had five children, but three of them died as infants.

During Revolutionary times John Dickinson puzzled many people by what seemed to be his inconsistent behavior. In 1767–68 he wrote the *Farmer's Letters*, a series of essays protesting British injustice. Later, while representing Pennsylvania in the Continental Congress, he wrote so many papers for Congress that Dickinson became known as the Penman of the Revolution. Yet he refused to vote for independence in July 1776. Dickinson then further surprised people by becoming one of only a few congressmen who actually fought for independence, serving at the Battle of Brandywine in Pennsylvania.

Americans were mystified. How could Dickinson write anti-British essays and fight the British, yet refuse to vote for independence? The answer was that he personally felt America was not ready to separate from England, yet he considered the majority opinion "sacred." As one of his country's best writers, he felt obligated to express Congress's views even when they opposed his own, and since America was at war, he wanted to serve with his countrymen.

Dickinson continued his remarkable career as the war ended. From 1781 to 1782 he was governor of Delaware, and from 1782 to 1785 he was governor of Pennsylvania, his other home state. For two months he was governor of both states at the same time! Representing Delaware, he served as chairman of the Annapolis Convention in 1786, and the next year the Delaware legislature appointed him to attend the Constitutional Convention.

Although he had written the first draft of the Articles of Confederation, Dickinson knew that a stronger central government was essential. At the Philadelphia convention he was especially concerned with how the country's lawmakers would be chosen, and he approved of the method that was adopted: House members would be elected by the people, while senators would be chosen by the state legis-

latures. (Amendment 17 changed this in 1913 by providing for the direct election of senators by the people.)

Unlike the thirty-eight other founders, Dickinson didn't exactly *sign* the Constitution. Suffering from exhaustion, he left the convention early but arranged for George Read, his old friend from his days in John Moland's law office, to sign for him. Back home, Dickinson wrote for the *Delaware Gazette* a series of letters supporting the Constitution. The new government would succeed, Dickinson claimed, because "the power of the people pervades the proposed system." His influence helped Delaware and Pennsylvania become the first two states to approve the Constitution.

Among his other achievements, John Dickinson worked to end slavery and educate poor children and helped found Pennsylvania's Dickinson College, which was named for him. The Penman of the Revolution died at his home in Wilmington, Delaware, on February 14, 1808, at the age of seventy-five.

GEORGE READ
"Do Away with States Altogether"

Geo. Read

BORN NEAR THE VILLAGE of North East in Maryland's Cecil County on September 18, 1733, George Read moved with his family to New Castle, Delaware, as a very young child. He attended an academy in New London, Pennsylvania, where his classmates included Thomas McKean and Charles Thomson. At about fifteen, George began studying in the office of attorney John Moland in Philadelphia, a city where he started his law practice five years later. Philadelphia had an abundance of attorneys, though, so he soon returned to New Castle. In an era when attorneys were generally distrusted, Read won the respect of New Castle's people, who called him the Honest Lawyer.

George Read was so intent on dedicating his life to his career that he decided not to marry. His plans changed when he fell in love with a widow named Gertrude Ross Till. George and Gertrude were married in January 1763. The couple had five children—four sons and a daughter.

In 1765, Read was elected to the Delaware legislature, where he served for many years, and from 1774 to 1777 he represented Delaware in the Continental Congress. For a long time Read believed that the thirteen colonies and the Mother Country could settle their differences peacefully. But once independence was proclaimed he thought Delaware should stand united with the rest of the country, so he signed the Declaration of Independence. He had close ties to three of the Declaration's other signers. Pennsylvanian George Ross (uncle to famed flag maker Betsy Ross) was his wife's brother. Delaware signer Thomas McKean had been his schoolmate, as had Charles Thomson, who signed not as a delegate but as secretary of the Continental Congress.

Read had a close call during the Revolution. In 1777 the British seized Delaware's governor, John McKinly, and Read learned that he was needed back home to take over the position. The Reads left Philadelphia, but were captured by British troops while making their way home. Fortunately Read convinced the enemy soldiers that he was a local man of no importance. The British released the family, and George Read went on to serve as Delaware's governor from late 1777 to March 1778.

The Honest Lawyer represented Delaware at the Annapolis Convention of 1786 and at the Constitutional Convention the next year. In Philadelphia, Read was a leading champion for the rights of the small states, at one point threatening to leave the convention if they weren't treated fairly. The United States should "do away with states altogether, and unite them all into one society," he asserted on another occasion. In the end, his colleagues didn't approve the proposal to get rid of states, and Read didn't walk out of the convention. He signed the Constitu-

tion (on the day before his fifty-fourth birthday) feeling that it was far from perfect but would help improve the country.

Actually, Read was the only man to sign the Constitution *twice*—once for himself and once for fellow Delawarean John Dickinson, who had left because of illness. Read then fought successfully for Delaware to ratify the Constitution and become the First State.

George Read was elected as one of Delaware's first two U.S. senators. He served from 1789 to 1793, when he resigned to become chief justice of the First State's supreme court. He still headed Delaware's highest court when he died in New Castle on September 21, 1798, just three days after his sixty-fifth birthday.

GUNNING BEDFORD JR.
"I Do Not, Gentlemen, Trust You"

Gunning Bedford jun

THE FIFTH OF ELEVEN CHILDREN, Gunning Bedford Jr. was born in Philadelphia sometime in 1747. He attended the Philadelphia Academy, then enrolled at Princeton College, where his classmates included James Madison of Virginia. While in college, Bedford married Jane Ballereau Parker. It was said that the first of the couple's five children attended Gunning's college graduation as a baby.

Gunning Bedford studied with a Philadelphia attorney in the early 1770s before opening his own law practice in 1774. During the Revolutionary War he briefly served as an aide to General George Washington. Many years later a pair of pistols were found among Bedford's effects. Bedford's family explained that General Washington had given him the pistols for protection when sending him on a dangerous secret mission from Trenton, New Jersey, to New York.

In about 1779 Bedford and his family moved to Delaware, settling first in Dover and later in the Wilmington region. From 1784 to 1789 he served as attorney general (chief law officer) of Delaware. Also in the 1780s he represented Delaware in the Continental Congress and held a seat in the Delaware legislature.

Delaware sent Bedford to Philadelphia as part of its delegation to the 1787 convention. Tall and heavyset, he was said to be the largest man at the gathering. He was also one of the boldest spokesmen for the rights of the small states.

"I do not, gentlemen, trust you!" he told the large-state delegates, while accusing them of trying to gang up on the small states. "If you possess the power, the abuse of it could not be checked!"

Bedford had another shock for his fellow delegates. If they didn't receive a fair deal, the small states might withdraw from the country and join up with some foreign nation. Bedford was playing dirty politics, his colleagues felt, yet his

threats helped convince the convention to grant the small states equal representation in the Senate.

After signing the Constitution, Bedford served as a delegate to the Delaware
convention that ratified the document less than three months later. Two years after that in 1789 his old commander, President George Washington, appointed
Bedford as a federal judge for the First State. He held this position for the last
twenty-three years of his life.

Judge Bedford spent his later years working on behalf of two good causes. He
promoted education in his state, serving as president of the trustees of Wilmington Academy. He also worked to end slavery, becoming a leading member of the
Delaware Society for Promoting the Abolition of Slavery. Gunning Bedford Jr.
died in Wilmington at the age of about sixty-five on March 30, 1812.

JACOB BROOM
"A Plain Good Man"

AT A POINT WHEN the convention had nearly dissolved without producing a new constitution, a quiet delegate from Delaware stepped forward to save the day.

Jacob Broom was born sometime in 1752 in Wilmington, Delaware. His family farmed, as most colonists did then, and his father also worked as a blacksmith. Jacob studied law and surveying at the school that became the College of Wilmington. At twenty-one he married a neighbor named Rachel Pierce, with whom he would have eight children.

In the 1700s, as today, people often had to work at several jobs to make ends meet. Jacob farmed. He worked as a surveyor—a person who determines land boundaries and dimensions. He also became a prosperous businessman. While still in his twenties, he entered politics. Among his many local offices, he was a justice of the peace and served on the board that oversaw Wilmington's water supply, sewage system, and streets.

Broom favored independence, but he would not fight in the Revolution due to the influence of his many friends and relatives who were Quakers—a faith that strongly opposed war. Instead, he aided the cause by becoming a surveyor for the Continental Army. Broom made detailed maps of the region for General Washington before the American forces fought the Battle of Brandywine in Pennsylvania in 1777.

In 1784 Jacob Broom was elected to the Delaware legislature, serving for about three years. He was chosen as one of Delaware's five delegates to the Constitutional Convention of 1787. Georgian William Pierce, who didn't sign the Constitution but provided a great service by writing character sketches of his fellow delegates, described Broom as "a plain good Man, with some abilities, but nothing to render him conspicuous; silent in public but cheerful and conversable in private."

Like everyone else, Broom didn't get everything he wanted at the convention. His proposal that his hometown of Wilmington, Delaware, be made the national capital was defeated, as was his suggestion that presidents serve for life unless voted out for misconduct. The decision to have two senators from each state was a major victory for Broom and the small states, but it didn't come easily.

As the large- and small-state delegates argued, their hostility for one another increased until on July 16 some men wanted to adjourn the convention for an unspecified period without picking a date for reopening. Had that happened, the delegates might have gone home, and the convention might have ended without producing a constitution.

Suddenly Jacob Broom leaped to his feet. They must not part in anger without producing a constitution, he insisted. Coming from the gentlemanly and soft-spoken Delawarean, this speech convinced the delegates to work out their disagreements. Some historians credit Jacob Broom with saving the convention.

After signing the Constitution, Broom withdrew from the national stage and returned to Delaware, where he served his state in many ways. In 1790 President Washington appointed him as Wilmington's first postmaster. He worked to establish bridges and canals in his state, and in 1795 he became chairman of the board of directors of the Delaware Bank.

Jacob Broom died in Philadelphia on April 25, 1810, at the age of about fifty-eight. In his will he left a large sum of money to a school for black children and to other benevolent causes.

RICHARD BASSETT
Founder of a Political Dynasty

Richard Bassett

RICHARD BASSETT WAS BORN in Cecil County, Maryland, on April 2, 1745. When Richard was a child, his father, a tavernkeeper, abandoned the family. In those days, when few women had jobs, it was often impossible for a single mother to support her children. Unable to care for him properly, his mother turned Richard over to a relative, Peter Lawson, who raised him. Lawson trained his adopted son to be an attorney like himself.

At about the age of twenty-five, Bassett moved to the Dover, Delaware, area, where he practiced law and farmed. He prospered, eventually owning a number of slaves and two estates in Delaware and one in Maryland. In 1774 Bassett married Ann Ennals, a Maryland woman. The couple had two daughters.

The year after Richard and Ann were married, the Revolution began. Bassett joined the army, and as captain of a troop of cavalry (horse soldiers), he fought under George Washington. On one occasion during the war, Bassett was entertaining a judge from Maryland at his home in Dover when a mob came to his door. The judge was a Loyalist (British sympathizer), the mob shouted, and ordered Bassett to turn him over for punishment. Brandishing his sword and pistol, Bassett told the mob that his friend was no Loyalist, and they would have to kill him to seize the man. Seeing Captain Bassett's determination to protect his friend, the mob backed off and headed home.

Bassett didn't serve as a soldier for long. In 1776 he was elected to the Delaware legislature, where he served for more than a decade. Having grown to hate slavery, he introduced an act to the legislature intended to make it easier for Delawareans to free slaves and to protect the rights of liberated slaves. Bassett's proposals became law in 1787. Bassett also freed his own slaves, and tried but failed to eliminate slavery in Delaware altogether. Slavery would continue in Delaware, and in several other states, until the Civil War ended the evil practice in 1865.

Meanwhile, in September 1786 Bassett had represented Delaware at the Annapolis Convention. He also represented the little state at the Constitutional Convention the following year. Although he made no noteworthy speeches, Bassett signed the Constitution. After returning home, he was instrumental in convincing his state's leaders to approve the document before anyone else.

In October 1788 Bassett and fellow founder George Read were chosen as Delaware's first U.S. senators. Bassett served in the Senate from 1789 to 1793. During that period lawmakers tackled the question of where to locate the nation's permanent national capital. Richard Bassett had the honor of casting the first vote in favor of a site on the Potomac River, where Washington, D.C., was subsequently built. From 1799 to 1801 Richard Bassett served as governor of the First State.

Following the death of his wife Ann, Bassett married a second time. He and his second wife, Betsy Garnett, had no children. Through his daughter Ann, however, Bassett began a political dynasty. Ann's husband, James Bayard, served as a U.S. senator from the First State. Richard Bassett's grandsons, James Bayard Jr. and Richard Bayard, also represented the little state in the Senate, as did his great-grandson Thomas Bayard and his great-great-grandson Thomas Bayard Jr.

The man who had helped Delaware become the First State died at his Maryland estate at the age of seventy. Some claim his date of death was August 16, 1815, while others insist it was September 15 of that year.

II. PENNSYLVANIA

The region that became Pennsylvania was claimed by Sweden and the Netherlands before England took over in 1664. In 1681 England's king gave the territory to Englishman William Penn. To honor the Penn family, the king named the colony Pennsylvania, meaning "Penn's woods."

William Penn belonged to the Religious Society of Friends, popularly known as the Quakers, a faith that was persecuted in England. Penn established his colony as a place where not only Quakers but other persecuted people, including Catholics and Jews, were welcome. In 1682 Penn founded Philadelphia, which grew into one of the great cities of the thirteen colonies.

Pennsylvania was the site of some key events of the Revolution. The Declaration of Independence was issued at Philadelphia's Independence Hall. George Washington's army survived the terrible winter of 1777–78 camped at Valley Forge, Pennsylvania. The battles of Brandywine and Germantown were fought in Pennsylvania. Philadelphia was the nation's capital on and off for a total of about sixteen years between 1776 and 1800.

With 400,000 people, Pennsylvania in 1787 was second only to Virginia in population among the thirteen states. As the host state, Pennsylvania had the most delegates—eight—at the Constitutional Convention. All eight signed the document, including world-famous Benjamin Franklin.

On December 12, 1787, Pennsylvania became the second state to approve the Constitution. Because it was located near the middle of the original thirteen states, much like the keystone at the center of an arch, Pennsylvania was nicknamed the Keystone State. Not until 1812 did Harrisburg become Pennsylvania's capital, as it remains today. In the years before the Civil War, many Pennsylvanians helped slaves escape along the Underground Railroad.

PENNSYLVANIA

Name	Birth Date	Age at Signing	Marriage(s)	Children	Death Date	Age at Death
BENJAMIN FRANKLIN*	January 17, 1706	81	Deborah Read	2	April 17, 1790	84
JAMES WILSON*	September 14, 1742	45	Rachel Bird Hannah Gray	7	August 21, 1798	55
GOUVERNEUR MORRIS	January 31, 1752	35	Anne Cary Randolph	1	November 6, 1816	64
ROBERT MORRIS*	January 31, 1734	53	Mary White	7	May 8, 1806	72
GEORGE CLYMER*	March 16, 1739	48	Elizabeth Meredith	8	January 23, 1813	73
THOMAS MIFFLIN	January 10, 1744	43	Sarah Morris	1	January 20, 1800	56
JARED INGERSOLL	October 27, 1749	37	Elizabeth Pettit	4	October 31, 1822	73
THOMAS FITZSIMONS	1741	About 46	Catharine Meade	0	August 26, 1811	About 70

*An asterisk (*) after a founder's name indicates that he also signed the Declaration of Independence.

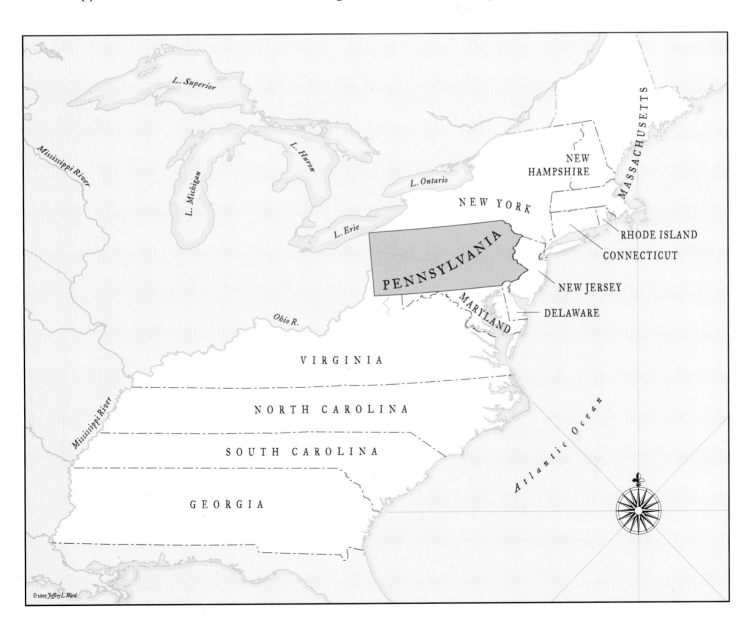

BENJAMIN FRANKLIN
The Remarkable Ben

B Franklin

THE FIFTEENTH OF SEVENTEEN CHILDREN, Benjamin Franklin was born in Boston, Massachusetts, on January 17, 1706. His family made and sold candles and soap at their shop, called the Blue Ball, next to their home. Ben entered school at the age of eight. He failed arithmetic but loved to read, often sitting up most of the night with a book. He also loved outdoors activities, particularly swimming and kite-flying. The first of his many inventions was for swimmers: four paddles that slipped over the feet and hands, helping the wearer swim faster.

Ben was pulled out of school at the age of ten and put to work in the family shop. He disliked making candles, though, so at twelve he was apprenticed to his brother, James, a printer nine years older than himself. As an apprentice, Ben was to work for his brother without pay for nine years while he learned the printer's trade. When Ben turned twenty-one, he could go out on his own as a printer.

James Franklin taught Ben how to print booklets, songs, and newspapers. But James beat Ben when he made mistakes and beat him some more when he talked back. Finally, Ben had had enough. A friend helped him stow away on a ship, and in the fall of 1723 the seventeen-year-old runaway apprentice sailed to New York City. He couldn't find a job as a printer there, so he continued on to Philadelphia, Pennsylvania, making half the hundred-mile journey by boat and the other half on foot. In Philadelphia Ben found work with a printer and did so well that he was soon running the business.

Ben went into the printing business for himself in 1728, and the next year he began his own newspaper, the *Pennsylvania Gazette*. A few years later he began his own almanac. Called *Poor Richard's Almanac*, it popularized numerous sayings, such as "A penny saved is a penny earned," "Little strokes fell great oaks," and "Great talkers, little doers."

In 1730 Ben married Deborah Read, with whose family he had lived upon first arriving in Philadelphia. Ben and Debby had a son named Franky, who died of smallpox at the age of four, and a daughter named Sally. Debby also helped Ben raise William Franklin, his son by another woman. Debby was of great help to Ben in his printing business. With her assistance, the *Pennsylvania Gazette* and *Poor Richard's Almanac* became America's leading newspaper and most popular almanac.

Ben had many other interests besides printing. He became a renowned scientist. In June 1752 he and his twenty-one-year-old son William flew a kite in a storm. Lightning struck the kite and made a spark, proving that lightning was electricity. Ben also became a famous inventor. He invented the lightning rod to protect people and buildings from lightning, bifocal glasses to help people see both near and far, a heating device called the Franklin stove, a musical instru-

ment with different-sized glass bowls called the glass harmonica, and an artificial arm that he used for taking books off high shelves.

In addition, Franklin helped make Philadelphia a great city. In 1731 he founded the Library Company of Philadelphia, which contributed to the establishment of America's library system. Five years later he founded the Union Fire Company, America's first volunteer fire department. In 1751 he helped start the Pennsylvania Hospital, the first general hospital in the thirteen colonies. That same year a school opened that Ben helped establish. Called the Philadelphia Academy, it later became the University of Pennsylvania.

By the Revolutionary War era Ben was so famous for his electrical experiments that rumors swept England about his amazing powers. Franklin had built an electrical machine that would flip all of England upside down like a pancake! Another device of his would burn England to a crisp! No such weapons existed, but Franklin did help Thomas Jefferson create the Declaration of Independence and then helped win independence by persuading France to join the American side in 1778.

From 1785 to 1788 Franklin served as Pennsylvania's governor. By 1787 Governor Franklin was past eighty years old and in such failing health that he sometimes had to be carried through Philadelphia in a chair. Nonetheless, his mind was still sharp and his prestige so great that few people would have considered holding the Constitutional Convention without him.

He was a key figure in the convention's success. When tempers flared, Franklin told funny stories to ease the tension. He was one of several delegates who argued for the Connecticut Compromise. And he helped convince delegates who were hesitant about signing the Constitution that they should do so for the sake of unity. At eighty-one, Benjamin Franklin was the oldest of the thirty-nine signers. He was also the only Founding Father whose fame equaled that of George Washington.

One of Ben's last projects was to try to end slavery. He served as the president of an antislavery society, and signed an address to Congress asking that slavery be outlawed. The famous statesman, scientist, inventor, and author died in Philadelphia on April 17, 1790, at the age of eighty-four.

JAMES WILSON
"The Best Form of Government"

James Wilson

JAMES WILSON WAS BORN in Scotland on September 14, 1742. His parents intended Jamie for the ministry, but his father's death forced him to withdraw from divinity school. Over the next several years Jamie worked as a tutor, but he disliked the job. Next he studied to become an accountant with little enthusiasm. Finally, Jamie decided that he needed a fresh start in life. His mother reluctantly gave her consent, and he sailed to America in 1765.

The young man from Scotland settled in Philadelphia, where he studied under eminent attorney John Dickinson. In 1767 Wilson became an attorney himself, and three years later he moved to Carlisle, Pennsylvania, to practice law. The next year, 1771, he married Rachel Bird, a wealthy young Pennsylvanian. James and Rachel had six children, including a son who was given the unusual name Bird Wilson.

James Wilson sided with his adopted country in its struggle with England. In 1774 he published a pamphlet in which he asserted that "all power is derived from the people—their happiness is the end of government." Since the Americans didn't want to be ruled by Britain any longer, Wilson argued, it was their right to break away. Elected to the Continental Congress in 1775, Wilson had the honor of signing the Declaration of Independence for Pennsylvania.

But his greatest achievement occurred at the Constitutional Convention of 1787. Wilson spoke on 168 occasions at the gathering, more than any other delegate except Gouverneur Morris. Early in the convention he compared the government to a pyramid, which must rest on the broadest base possible: the American public. "No government can long subsist without the confidence of the people," Wilson declared.

Some delegates wanted future states in the West to have less of a say in government than the thirteen original states. That was unfair, argued Wilson, whose colleagues agreed. Some delegates wanted the national legislature to elect the president. No, said Wilson, the people should elect the president. Again, his colleagues agreed, although the Electoral College was also created to help decide presidential elections.

However, Wilson argued in vain that the people should elect both houses of Congress. The people would elect the House of Representatives, the convention decided, but the state legislatures would select the Senate. Only after the Seventeenth Amendment was ratified in 1913 did Americans begin to elect their U.S. senators, as Wilson had wanted.

Following the convention, Wilson worked for Pennsylvania's ratification. In one speech the tall Pennsylvanian with the thick glasses called the new constitution "the best form of government which has ever been offered to the world." Wilson's efforts were instrumental in Pennsylvania's early approval of the Constitution.

In 1789 the first president, George Washington, appointed Wilson to be one of the country's first Supreme Court justices, a position he held for the rest of his

life. His last years were troubled, though. Rachel Wilson died in 1786 at the age of thirty-nine. In 1793 Wilson married Hannah Gray. They had one son, but he died in infancy. During the 1790s Wilson also made unwise business deals. As happened to many people who owed money in those days, he was imprisoned for debt, first in New Jersey and then in North Carolina. James Wilson died in poverty at the age of fifty-five on August 21, 1798, in Edenton, North Carolina.

GOUVERNEUR MORRIS
"We the People of the United States"

GOUVERNEUR MORRIS WAS BORN at Morrisania, an estate in what is now New York City, on January 31, 1752. His unusual first name honored his mother, whose maiden name had been Sarah Gouverneur. His father was a judge whose family had long been among the wealthiest and most prominent New Yorkers.

While attending the academy Benjamin Franklin had helped establish in Philadelphia, Gouverneur exercised his lifelong love of jokes and pranks. He and his classmates would close their classroom shutters, lock their Latin teacher in with them, and in the darkened room shout and throw books at him. The teacher had to hide beneath a desk repeatedly before school authorities discovered what was going on and put a stop to it.

Morris was a student at King's College (now Columbia University) in New York City when he suffered a terrible accident. He scalded his right arm so badly that he had to take a year off from his studies. Still, he managed to graduate in 1768 at the age of sixteen. He then studied law and was admitted to the bar when he was only nineteen.

His disfigured arm prevented Morris from fighting for independence, so instead he served in New York's revolutionary government, surprising many people with his democratic ideas. Morris helped craft a new constitution for New York that offered a great deal of religious toleration for its time. He also tried to abolish slavery in New York, arguing that "every human being who breathes the air of this State should enjoy the privileges of a freeman." Unfortunately, New York didn't outlaw slavery until 1827.

Although he was only in his mid-twenties, Morris was sent to represent New York at the Continental Congress in 1778–79. He wrote many papers for Congress, predicting in one that the United States would be a refuge "to mankind;

America shall receive and comfort the oppressed, the miserable, and the poor of every nation."

Defeated for reelection to Congress in 1779, Morris moved to Pennsylvania and began practicing law in Philadelphia. Not long after the move he was driving his carriage when his horses went out of control, and he was suddenly thrown from the vehicle. The doctors of the time couldn't save his severely injured left leg. They amputated it, and Morris was fitted with a wooden leg.

The fact that he had an artificial leg and a damaged arm didn't stop Morris from enjoying an active and full life. Well over six feet in height and very strong, the "Tall Boy," as he was nicknamed, enjoyed horseback riding, fishing, canoeing, and taking walks of up to ten miles.

Pennsylvania elected the transplanted New Yorker to attend the Constitutional Convention. There he made 173 speeches—the most of any delegate—yet often wound up on the losing side. For example, he preferred that the president and senators hold their offices for life, but their terms were made four and six years, respectively.

He also spoke eloquently against slavery at the convention. It was evil, he declared, for "the inhabitant of Georgia or South Carolina to go to the coast of Africa and tear away his fellow creatures from their dearest connections and damn them to the most cruel bondages." The convention decided to allow the slave trade to continue until 1808 or later, however.

Gouverneur Morris was named to the five-man Committee on Style assigned to write the Constitution. Morris did most of the writing, and was largely responsible for the magnificent fifty-two-word preamble in which the nation received the name we know it by, with an uppercase *U* and *S*:

> We the People of the United States, in Order to form a more perfect Union, establish Justice, insure domestic Tranquility, provide for the common defense, promote the general Welfare, and secure the Blessings of Liberty to ourselves and our Posterity, do ordain and establish this Constitution for the United States of America.

The new framework of government was not perfect, Gouverneur Morris said after its completion. But despite its faults, he believed it was "the best [constitution] that was to be attained."

The year after the Constitutional Convention, Gouverneur Morris sailed for Europe. He spent nearly a decade overseas, serving part of the time as U.S. minister to France. He returned to his old home, Morrisania, in January 1799. The next year he was elected as one of New York's U.S. senators. In the Senate he supported the Louisiana Purchase—the deal with France by which the United States obtained territory that later became fifteen states.

On Christmas Day of 1809 Gouverneur Morris married Anne Cary Randolph of Virginia. The bride was thirty-five and the groom almost fifty-eight years old. He and Anne had one child, a son named Gouverneur Morris Jr., who was born in 1813 when Morris was sixty-one. Gouverneur Morris lived only three more years. He died at Morrisania on November 6, 1816, about three months before what would have been his sixty-fifth birthday. The man who had written the Constitution reportedly said on his deathbed: "Sixty-five years ago it pleased the Almighty to call me into existence here, on this spot, in this very room. And how shall I complain that He is pleased to call me hence?"

ROBERT MORRIS
"The Work of Plain, Honest Men"

Rob Morris

ROBERT MORRIS WAS BORN in or near Liverpool, England, on January 31, 1734. Nothing is known about his mother. His father moved to America around 1738. "Bob" followed when he was thirteen, and went to work for Philadelphia merchant Charles Willing. In 1750 Bob's father died in a freak shooting accident, leaving the sixteen-year-old youth an orphan.

Thanks to his keen business sense, young Morris made his way in the world with amazing success. Around the age of twenty he became a partner in Willing & Morris, a firm that owned ships and imported and exported goods. He was associated with the company for about forty years, becoming one of America's richest people. In 1769 Morris married a Maryland woman named Mary White. The couple had five sons and two daughters, raising them at their country estate, The Hills, outside Philadelphia.

Elected to the Continental Congress in 1775, Morris opposed independence when the Revolution began. But once the decision was made to separate from England, he signed the Declaration of Independence and dedicated his life to what he called "the service of my country." Congress appointed him superintendent of finance, which meant that he had to raise money to pay for the war. One way he did this was by establishing the Bank of North America— the first national bank in the United States—which issued its own printed money called "Long Bobs" and "Short Bobs," named for him. At times the "Financier of the Revolution" spent his own funds on food, supplies, and salaries for the American troops. To finance the Battle of Yorktown, fought in Virginia in 1781, he reportedly spent a *million* dollars out of his own pocket.

Morris represented Pennsylvania at the Annapolis Convention in 1786, and at the Constitutional Convention the following year. After the meeting opened, Morris nominated George Washington to serve as president of the convention, and, along with John Rutledge of South Carolina, escorted Washington to the president's chair. George Washington lived with Morris and his family during the convention in Philadelphia, and the two men sometimes went fishing together during breaks in the deliberations.

Although he was rather quiet at the convention, Morris appreciated the importance of the proceedings. Writing to two of his sons while the convention was in session, he pointed out: "You, my children, ought to pray for a successful issue to [our] labors, as the result is to be a form of government under which you are to live." After signing the Constitution, Morris wrote to a friend that the document was "the work of plain, honest men."

Robert Morris served as a U.S. senator from Pennsylvania under the new government from 1789 to 1795. Meanwhile, he had spent a fortune on real estate. He accumulated a great deal of land in Washington, D.C., as well as millions of acres in New York State. Partly because he had spent so much of his own money helping to win the Revolution, he fell into debt and couldn't even pay his taxes on his

vast holdings. Robert Morris spent three and a half years in "Prune Street," the Philadelphia debtors' prison.

Morris was finally released in August 1801 when he was sixty-seven years old. His health had suffered during his years in prison, and by the time of his release he was broken in both body and spirit. Forgotten by younger Americans who knew little about his contributions to their country, Robert Morris lived his last five years in poverty. The "Financier of the Revolution" died on May 8, 1806, at the age of seventy-two.

GEORGE CLYMER

"Our Country Possesses a Greater Proportion of Liberty"

Geo. Clymer

GEORGE CLYMER WAS BORN in Philadelphia on March 16, 1739. He had an older sister and brother, but neither survived early childhood. His mother died when he was just over a year old, followed by his father when George was seven. The orphan was placed in the care of a childless aunt and uncle who provided him with a fine education and business training. By the age of twenty-one, George had become a successful merchant.

A Philadelphia business associate of Clymer's named Reese Meredith had a daughter named Elizabeth who caught George's eye. Two days after his twenty-sixth birthday, George married Elizabeth Meredith. The couple enjoyed forty-seven years of marriage and had eight children. It also appears that Clymer fathered a child with another woman prior to his marriage.

During the Revolution, Clymer helped supply the American forces with gunpowder and food and while serving in the Continental Congress became one of nine Pennsylvanians to sign the Declaration of Independence. Fearing for his family's safety, he moved them to a safer spot in Pennsylvania's Chester County, beyond the reach of the British. It was said that Clymer would leave Philadelphia late in the afternoon, ride twenty-five miles to visit his wife and children, and then gallop back to attend Congress early the next morning.

From 1785 to 1788 Clymer held a seat in the Pennsylvania legislature. At a time when there was a bias against foreign-born people living in the United States, Clymer insisted that they must be allowed their rights. "As our country possesses a greater proportion of liberty than any other on this earth," he said, it should be a refuge for people from other lands. His fellow lawmakers agreed, and Pennsylvania passed a law to protect its foreign-born residents.

A convention was needed to revise the national government, Clymer also told the state legislature. As one of Pennsylvania's delegates, he worked on parts of the new framework of government relating to finances and became one of only six men who signed both the Declaration of Independence and the Constitution. Clymer then helped win ratification of the Constitution in Pennsylvania.

Clymer was elected as one of Pennsylvania's first members of the House of Representatives, where he served from 1789 to 1791. Congressman Clymer fought for the rights of foreign-born Americans to own property, vote, and hold office. He also argued that Philadelphia should be named the permanent capital of the United States, but that honor went to Washington, D.C.

In 1796, at President Washington's request, George Clymer made a nearly 1,000-mile journey to Georgia where he helped negotiate a treaty with the Creek Indians. Unlike most Americans of his time, Clymer was so intent on being fair to the Native Americans that he angered three officials from Georgia who were involved in the negotiations.

George Clymer, who once wrote to his son Henry that he hated the thought of retirement, remained active until the end of his life. He spent his last years as a trustee for the University of Pennsylvania and as president of the Philadelphia Bank. Seventy-three-year-old George Clymer died on January 23, 1813, at the home of his son Henry outside Philadelphia.

THOMAS MIFFLIN
"Are You Willing to Serve Your Country to Save Your Constitution?"

Thomas Mifflin

THOMAS MIFFLIN WAS BORN into a well-to-do Quaker family in Philadelphia on January 10, 1744. He attended a Quaker school before entering what is now the University of Pennsylvania at the age of about twelve—remarkably young even by the standards of the 1700s, when students typically entered college at fifteen or sixteen. Judging by doodles he made in a notebook, his mind sometimes wandered from his studies. He drew pictures of ships, birds, and hands, and practiced signing his name in fancy ways. Still, he concentrated well enough to graduate from college at sixteen.

To prepare for a business career, Thomas spent four years working in a Philadelphia countinghouse, an institution similar to a modern bank, and then traveled in Europe for a year. Most young Americans who went abroad were impressed by European culture, but young Mifflin declared that his travels made him "better pleased" with his country than before he left.

Back in Philadelphia, Mifflin entered the merchant business with his younger brother George. The Mifflin brothers made a great deal of money buying and selling goods. In the early spring of 1767, the rising young merchant married his cousin Sarah Morris, with whom he had one child, a daughter named Emily.

By the time of Mifflin's marriage, the thirteen colonies and Britain were clashing over taxes and other issues. In 1772, twenty-eight-year-old Thomas Mifflin decided to run for a seat in Pennsylvania's colonial legislature. He was an eloquent spokesman for America's rights, and he had another quality that won him many followers. In an era when wealthy people generally associated only with each other, Mifflin enjoyed the company of the city's mechanics, as laborers were called. The poorer people adored Thomas Mifflin, who began a long career of public service by winning the election.

In the spring of 1775, when the news arrived that the war for independence had begun in Massachusetts, eight thousand people gathered in Philadelphia for a town meeting. Thomas Mifflin spoke to the huge crowd about the struggle that lay ahead:

> Let us not be bold in declarations, and afterwards cold in action. Let not the patriotic feelings of today be forgotten tomorrow, nor have it said of Philadelphia, that she passed noble resolutions, slept upon them, and afterwards neglected them.

Few people did as much as Mifflin to win independence. For a few months he was General George Washington's aide-de-camp or special military assistant. Washington also selected Mifflin to be the army's quartermaster general or officer responsible for obtaining clothing, food, and other essentials for the troops. In addition, he served as a soldier, fighting so gallantly at one skirmish that a witness claimed he "never saw a greater display of personal bravery than was exhibited in the conduct of Colonel Mifflin."

Besides all this, Mifflin served on and off in the Continental Congress, which

ran the country in its early years. In late 1783 he was elected president of Congress, making him in effect the nation's chief executive for about six months. He was president when Congress ratified the treaty ending the Revolutionary War in early 1784.

Mifflin was among those selected by the Pennsylvania legislature to attend the Constitutional Convention of 1787. Although he spoke just once at the convention, he signed the Constitution and helped convince his state's leaders to approve it three months later.

In 1788 Mifflin became the Keystone State's governor. He held the office for eleven years and was so well liked that in the 1790 election he defeated his opponent by an incredible ten-to-one margin! During his governorship, Pennsylvania was the scene of a national crisis. According to Article I, Section 8, of the Constitution, "The Congress shall have Power to lay and collect Taxes" and other revenues. Congress passed a law taxing liquor in 1791. This angered many western Pennsylvania farmers who earned part of their living by making and selling liquor. By 1794 they were defying the law, leading to clashes with government officials. President Washington wanted Governor Mifflin to send out the state militia to quell this Whiskey Rebellion, as it became known.

Although he sympathized with the farmers, Governor Mifflin realized that the law must be obeyed. He began raising troops to put down the rebellion. At Philadelphia's City Hall, he made a recruiting speech in which he asked, "Are you willing to serve your country to save your Constitution?" On September 26, 1794, he made another great speech in Lancaster, Pennsylvania, in which he explained that imperfect laws could be amended or repealed, but the Constitution must be obeyed if the United States was to last. Troops were raised, some rebels were arrested, and the uprising was ended.

Thomas Mifflin might have continued as Pennsylvania governor for many more years if he hadn't been limited to three terms by state law. He retired as governor in 1799 but couldn't stay away from politics. That year he was elected to the Pennsylvania House of Representatives, where he was serving when he died of a sudden illness on January 20, 1800, ten days after his fifty-sixth birthday. He had been so generous with his money that he was practically penniless at his death and had to be buried at the expense of the state of Pennsylvania.

JARED INGERSOLL
Like Father, Unlike Son

Jared Ingersoll

JARED INGERSOLL WAS BORN in New Haven, Connecticut, on October 27, 1749. His mother was Hannah Ingersoll, and his father a Yale-educated attorney named Jared Ingersoll Sr. Following in his father's footsteps, young Jared enrolled at Yale College in his hometown of New Haven. Like Thomas Mifflin, he was only about twelve when he entered college. He was a student at Yale when the British passed the Stamp Act of 1765, requiring Americans to buy special tax stamps for such items as newspapers, wills, marriage licenses, school diplomas, and playing cards.

Jared Sr. sided with Britain in the quarrel with America and agreed to distribute the tax stamps in Connecticut. Incensed at him, the colony's people held protest meetings and even burned a dummy that had been made to look like Ingersoll. In September 1765, Jared Sr. was riding on horseback between New Haven and Hartford when he was surrounded by angry patriots, some of them armed with clubs. The mob threatened him with their weapons, forcing him to quit as stamp distributor.

Young Jared shared his father's Loyalist opinions for quite a while. After graduating from Yale in 1766 at age sixteen, he sailed to England. He studied law in London before going to Paris, where he became friends with Benjamin Franklin, then representing the newly independent United States in France. Franklin may have influenced him to change his thinking, for by the time he returned home in 1778, Jared Ingersoll sided with America and opposed his father's views.

Jared Ingersoll settled in Philadelphia, the capital of the young country. In a city that was famous for its outstanding attorneys, Ingersoll won a reputation as one of the best. He was elected to serve in the Continental Congress in 1780. Late the following year he married Elizabeth Pettit. The couple had four children, all boys.

In 1787 the Pennsylvania legislature named Ingersoll to attend the Constitutional Convention. He said little during the discussions but was known to favor the creation of a stronger federal government. William Pierce of Georgia wrote that Ingersoll "speaks well and comprehends his subject fully," but that he had a "modesty that keeps him back" from greater participation. One of the rare times he addressed his fellow delegates was on September 17, the final day of the convention. After Ben Franklin proposed that the delegates sign the Constitution, Ingersoll stood up to support his elderly friend's suggestion.

Ingersoll served as Pennsylvania's attorney general, or chief law officer, from 1790 to 1799, and held that post again from 1811 to 1817. In 1812 he ran for vice president of the United States as the running mate of De Witt Clinton, the mayor of New York City. But Ingersoll's fellow founder James Madison of Virginia was reelected president, while Elbridge Gerry of Massachusetts became vice president.

Among the clients Ingersoll represented as a lawyer was Senator William

Blount, another fellow founder who got in trouble in the 1790s with his land deals and political schemes. In 1821, at the age of seventy-one, Ingersoll became presiding judge of the Philadelphia District Court, a position he held for the brief remainder of his life. The man who many years before had defied his father's wishes by siding with his country died on Halloween of 1822, four days after his seventy-third birthday.

THOMAS FITZSIMONS
He Went Broke Helping His Friends

Thos Fitzsimons

THOMAS FITZSIMONS WAS BORN in Ireland sometime in 1741. Not only is his precise date of birth unknown, historians disagree about the spelling of his last name. Besides FitzSimons, it has been spelled Fitzsimons, Fitzsimmons, and even Fitzsimmins. At the age of about nineteen Thomas sailed to America with his parents, his twin sister, and their three brothers. The family settled in Philadelphia, where Thomas found a job in a countinghouse. In 1763 he married Catharine Meade, the daughter of a wealthy merchant. The couple had no children. Thomas went into business with his wife's brother, and within a few years he was one of the most successful merchants in Philadelphia.

FitzSimons served America in many ways during the period of the country's birth. He was elected to Pennsylvania's new revolutionary government in 1774. In an age when religious discrimination was rampant, he was one of the first Catholics to hold public office in Pennsylvania. He also raised and commanded a company of militia that served in New Jersey in 1776–77. In addition, FitzSimons was a member of Pennsylvania's navy board, helping to construct ships for America's cause. Besides all this, in 1780 his firm provided several thousand dollars to feed and clothe the Continental Army, and the next year he helped Robert Morris establish the country's first national bank: the Bank of North America.

The Pennsylvania legislature sent FitzSimons to the Continental Congress in 1782–83, to the Annapolis Convention in 1786, and to the Constitutional Convention in 1787. FitzSimons seldom took part in the debates at the meeting in Philadelphia but supported the creation of a strong national government.

After the new constitution went into effect, FitzSimons was elected to the U.S. House of Representatives. For three terms, from 1789 to 1795, he represented the Keystone State in the House, specializing in financial issues.

In his later years, Thomas FitzSimons became known for his community service. He worked on behalf of education. In 1791—the year the school adopted its present name—he became a trustee for the University of Pennsylvania. He held this post for twenty years. FitzSimons was said to be the single largest contributor to the building of St. Augustine's Roman Catholic Church in Philadelphia. He was also the president of the Philadelphia Chamber of Commerce on several occasions.

It was said that FitzSimons was too kindhearted to turn away friends who came to him seeking money. He reportedly loaned hundreds of thousands of dollars to his friends, including Robert Morris. Sometimes they couldn't repay the loans. Bad land deals also cost FitzSimons a fortune. In 1805, at the age of sixty-four, he went bankrupt, but was able to avoid debtors' prison, unlike his friend Robert Morris. FitzSimons died in Philadelphia at the age of about seventy on August 26, 1811.

III. NEW JERSEY

Like Delaware and Pennsylvania, New Jersey was colonized by Dutch and Swedish settlers before the English seized the region in 1664. They named the colony New Jersey for England's Isle of Jersey.

In colonial days, its farms and gardens were so beautiful that New Jersey was referred to as "the Garden of North America." With American independence, New Jersey became known as the Garden State. Because nearly a hundred Revolutionary War battles and skirmishes were fought there, New Jersey also earned the nickname the Cockpit of the Revolution.

By 1787 New Jersey had 170,000 people. Only four states had a smaller population. At the Constitutional Convention, New Jersey's delegates argued for the rights of the small states. William Paterson presented the "New Jersey Plan." Had it been adopted, this scheme would have established a one-house legislature in which all thirteen states had an equal vote. Paterson and three other delegates signed the Constitution for New Jersey, which became the third state under the Constitution by approving the document on December 18, 1787.

Trenton became New Jersey's permanent capital in 1790. Although it still retains its old nickname, the Garden State today is also sometimes called the Workshop of the Nation because of its densely populated urban areas and extensive industries.

NEW JERSEY

Name	Birth Date	Age at Signing	Marriage(s)	Children	Death Date	Age at Death
WILLIAM LIVINGSTON	November 30, 1723	63	Susanna French	13	July 25, 1790	66
WILLIAM PATERSON	December 24, 1745	41	Cornelia Bell Euphemia White	3	September 9, 1806	60
DAVID BREARLEY	June 11, 1745	42	Elizabeth Mullen Betsy Higbee	7	August 16, 1790	45
JONATHAN DAYTON	October 16, 1760	26	Susannah Williamson	2	October 9, 1824	63

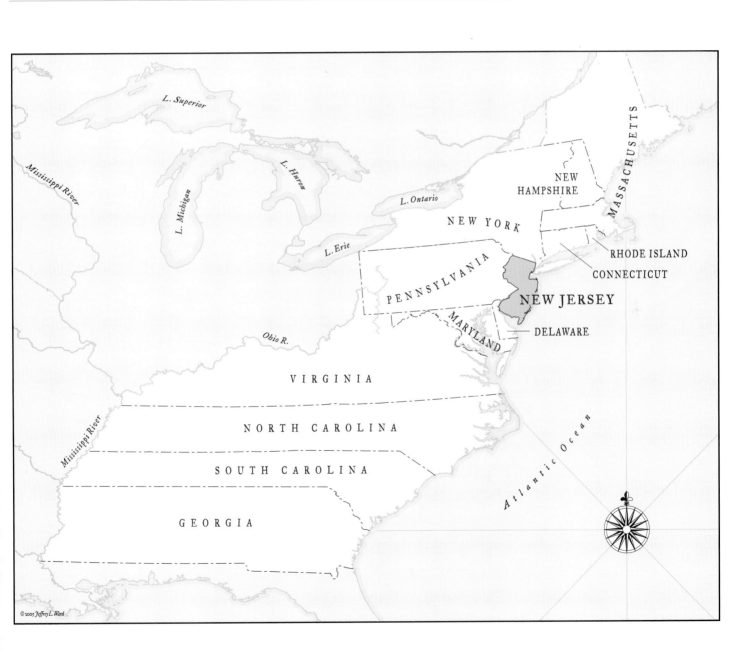

WILLIAM LIVINGSTON
"A New Constitution Which Promises National Happiness"

Wil: Livingston

WILLIAM LIVINGSTON WAS BORN into a wealthy family in Albany, New York, on November 30, 1723. He was raised mainly by his grandmother on his mother's side. According to family lore, she spoiled him so badly that he grew up expecting to always get his own way. Except for one year, William lived with his grandmother in Albany until he left for college. But what a year that was! At the age of twelve, William went with a missionary to live with New York's Mohawk Indians. This experience would prove helpful if he ever entered the fur trade or purchased land along the frontier, his family felt.

At thirteen William entered Connecticut's Yale College. After graduating, William, who loved to paint pictures, wanted to study art in Italy. But the Livingstons needed an attorney in the family, so William had to forget about art and become a lawyer.

Livingston fell in love with Susanna French of New Jersey, but his family insisted she wasn't rich enough and wouldn't grant William permission to marry her. Only after Susanna became pregnant with William's child did the couple marry. William and Susanna enjoyed nearly half a century of married life and had seven sons and six daughters. A doting husband and father, William claimed that he liked having thirteen children because that was the "number of the United States." Sadly, though, only seven of his children lived to adulthood.

Livingston finally became a lawyer in 1748 and practiced in both New York and New Jersey. He entered politics in the late 1750s. While serving in the New York legislature, he opposed the English government's interference in colonial matters. Livingston was also one of the first well-known American politicians to take a strong stand against slavery.

In the early 1770s William and his family moved to New Jersey, where he lived in semiretirement for a time. One day, a homeless youth appeared at Livingston's door bearing letters of introduction. Livingston befriended the young man, put him through school, and often invited him to his home. The youth was Alexander Hamilton, who many years later would be Livingston's colleague at the Constitutional Convention.

The Revolutionary War drew William Livingston back into public affairs. From 1774 to 1776 Livingston served in the Continental Congress and would have signed the Declaration of Independence (as his older brother Philip Livingston did for New York) if he hadn't had to take command of New Jersey militiamen in June 1776. That August he was elected as New Jersey's first state governor and served for fourteen years. During the war the British placed a price on his head, leading to numerous attempts to kill or kidnap him. His family had to scatter, and for about six years Livingston survived by moving from town to

town, never remaining for more than two straight nights in the same place. Amid these difficulties, he did his best to run his state and supply George Washington's army with troops.

Following the war, Governor Livingston worked to end slavery, which he called "disgraceful" among a people who claimed to "idolize liberty." He joined an antislavery society in 1786 and that same year steered through legislation banning the importation of slaves into New Jersey.

In the spring of 1787, sixty-three-year-old William Livingston was appointed as one of the Garden State's delegates to the Constitutional Convention. Because of his obligations as governor, he couldn't attend all of the sessions in Philadelphia, and when he was present he played only a small role in the debates. He had high hopes for the Constitution, however, and helped win New Jersey's ratification of the document on December 18, 1787.

Optimistic that the country would thrive under its new constitution, Livingston wrote to a friend in 1788, "I have lived to see adopted a new Constitution which promises national happiness." William Livingston served as New Jersey's governor until the end of his life. He died at Liberty Hall, his home in Elizabeth, New Jersey, on July 25, 1790, at the age of sixty-six.

WILLIAM PATERSON
"Father of the United States Senate"

BORN IN WHAT IS NOW Northern Ireland on Christmas Eve of 1745, William Paterson sailed to America with his family when he was not yet two years old. The Patersons settled in Princeton, New Jersey, where they opened a general store in their home. In 1756 Princeton College was established just a hundred paces from the Patersons' doorstep. As a child, William watched the Princeton students walking about in their caps and gowns and dreamed of attending the college one day, too.

William prepared by studying Greek and Latin at a local school, and was admitted to Princeton College at thirteen. He graduated four years later, then studied law under Richard Stockton, who would later sign the Declaration of Independence. In 1772 Paterson moved to Raritan, New Jersey, where he practiced law and became partners with his younger brother Thomas in a store.

The young lawyer hoped to live quietly, explaining that his goal was to "pass through life without much noise and bustle." The times wouldn't allow it. During the Revolution he served in New Jersey's legislature, helped create its first state constitution in 1776, worked to organize the state's war effort, and held office as New Jersey's attorney general.

Paterson also found time for romance. He fell in love with Cornelia Bell, a young neighbor whom he called "the sweetest pattern of female excellence." At the end of his long workdays he would stay up half the night writing love letters to her. The couple married in 1779 and had three children. Sadly, Cornelia and their year-old daughter both died in 1783. For a while, William raised his remaining daughter and son on his own. Then in 1785 he married Euphemia White, one of his deceased wife's closest friends.

In 1787 the New Jersey legislature chose Paterson to attend the Constitutional Convention, where he became the leading spokesman for the smaller states. On June 15 he presented the New Jersey Plan, which proposed that each state have an equal vote in a one-house legislature. Although it met defeat, the New Jersey Plan led to the Connecticut Compromise, which established one house, the Senate, having two members from each state. Fittingly, the man who has been called the Father of the U.S. Senate was elected as one of New Jersey's first U.S. senators in November 1789.

New Jersey's governor, William Livingston, died in 1790. Elected as the new governor, Paterson left the Senate and ran the Garden State from late 1790 until 1793, when President Washington named him to the U.S. Supreme Court. Paterson sat on the nation's highest court for his last thirteen years.

As time passed, Paterson's admiration for the U.S. Constitution grew. Near the end of his life, Justice Paterson delivered a Supreme Court opinion in

which he reminded Americans of the magnificence of their governmental framework:

> The law is no respecter of persons. It is inflexible and even-handed, and should not be subject to any improper considerations or views. This ought to be the case particularly in the United States, which we have been always led to consider as a government not of men, but of laws, of which the Constitution is the basis.

In the fall of 1803 Paterson was riding in his carriage when the vehicle went off the road and overturned. His wife and son, who were with him, escaped serious harm, but Paterson was severely injured and couldn't walk for weeks. His health deteriorated until his death at his daughter's home at Albany, New York, on September 9, 1806, at the age of sixty. The city of Paterson, New Jersey, was named for him.

DAVID BREARLEY
"Very Much in the Esteem of the People"

David Brearley.

DAVID BREARLEY (sometimes spelled Brearly) was born near Trenton, New Jersey, on June 11, 1745. He attended nearby Princeton but did not graduate from the college. Instead he studied law and opened a practice in Allentown, New Jersey, in 1767, the year he married Elizabeth Mullen. Elizabeth died after just ten years of marriage, but during that time she and David had four children.

In the Revolutionary era New Jersey had one of the highest percentages of Loyalists among the thirteen colonies. About half of all New Jerseyans sided with Britain. David Brearley, however, was such a patriot that even before the war British authorities arrested him for treason, an extremely serious crime that involved attempting to overthrow the government, and was sometimes punished by death. Fortunately for Brearley a mob of his fellow patriots rescued him from the clutches of the enemy.

Soon after the war began, Brearley volunteered to fight. He served with New Jersey troops at the battles of Brandywine and Germantown in Pennsylvania, and Monmouth in his home state of New Jersey. Brearley also helped draft New Jersey's first state constitution during the war. Adopted by New Jersey in 1776, this framework for state government remained in effect for sixty-eight years, until 1844.

In June 1779 the New Jersey legislature elected David Brearley chief justice of the state. He held the position for ten years, moving to Trenton during this period. He married again in 1783. With his second wife, Elizabeth "Betsy" Higbee, he had three children, making a total of seven in the Brearley family.

When a convention was scheduled to overhaul the nation's government, New Jersey was the first state to name its delegates, and David Brearley was the first delegate New Jersey selected. Brearley was "very much in the esteem of the people," his fellow delegate William Pierce of Georgia wrote. "As an orator he has little to boast of, but as a man he has every virtue."

At the convention Brearley was a spokesman for the New Jersey or Small-State Plan, which would have maintained Congress as it existed under the Articles of Confederation: a single house in which each state had one vote. Brearley also made an unusual proposal. Rather than let the big states dominate the little ones, the delegates should take a map of America, erase all the existing borders between the states, and create thirteen new states of equal size. Brearley's idea wasn't taken any more seriously than George Read's proposal to "do away with states altogether."

Once he lost his battle for one state, one vote, Brearley suggested that the House of Representatives be limited to sixty-five members. He won this point, and the original House was set at ten members for Virginia; eight each for Massachusetts and Pennsylvania; six each for New York and Maryland; five each for Connecticut, North Carolina, and South Carolina; four for New Jersey; three each for New Hampshire and Georgia; and one each for Rhode Island and Delaware. Later, the House membership rose as new states were admitted and the country's population grew. Then in 1929, legislation was passed fixing House membership at 435, which is the number it still has today.

After signing the Constitution, Brearley was elected president of New Jersey's ratification convention. Under his leadership, New Jersey became the third state on December 18, 1787. Two years later, President Washington appointed Brearley a federal judge for the Garden State. He served in that capacity for less than a year, dying at the age of only forty-five on August 16, 1790, in Trenton, New Jersey.

JONATHAN DAYTON
The Youngest Founding Father

Jona: Dayton

JONATHAN DAYTON WAS BORN in Elizabeth, New Jersey, on October 16, 1760. After attending school in his hometown, he enrolled in Princeton, the college William Paterson and David Brearley had attended. He graduated in 1776 but didn't go to the ceremony. As soon as his college studies ended, fifteen-year-old Jonathan Dayton joined the Continental Army. He rose to the rank of captain and served in campaigns in Pennsylvania, New York, and New Jersey. Captured in New Jersey in 1780, Dayton was held prisoner on New York's Staten Island for a short time, but was freed in a prisoner exchange. He fought in the war's final battle, the great American victory at Yorktown, Virginia, in the fall of 1781.

As the war ended, Jonathan married New Jerseyan Susannah Williamson, with whom he had two daughters. He studied law, becoming an attorney around 1786, and also operated a business with his father called E. Dayton and Son.

Elias Dayton, Jonathan's father, was chosen as one of New Jersey's representatives to the Constitutional Convention, but couldn't or didn't want to attend the meeting. Jonathan was then chosen to take his father's place. Just twenty-six years old, Jonathan Dayton was the youngest delegate at the convention. William Pierce of Georgia described him as a man "of Talents, with ambition." Dayton had a big flaw, he added: a quick "temper that is injurious to him."

Despite his youth, Dayton spoke frequently at the convention, arguing for the rights of New Jersey and the other small states. He wanted all the states to have equal representation in both the House and Senate, but his colleagues decided that only the Senate should be set up that way. Despite his opposition to some aspects of the Constitution, Dayton signed it on September 17, 1787. On the day of the signing, the youngest founder was twenty-nine days shy of his twenty-seventh birthday.

Dayton held office in both houses of Congress for the new nation. He represented the Garden State in the U.S. House of Representatives between 1791 and
1799, serving as Speaker of the House for about half that time. Between 1799 and
1805 he represented New Jersey in the U.S. Senate.

In the late 1700s and early 1800s many Americans bought land along the frontier. Jonathan Dayton invested in vast amounts of land in what is now Ohio. The
city of Dayton, Ohio, which was first settled in the 1790s, was named in his honor.
But in the year 1800 it was discovered that Dayton had dishonestly kept $18,000
of congressional funds for his own use. Although he repaid the money, Dayton
had damaged his reputation. Later he did something worse, becoming involved
with fellow New Jerseyan Aaron Burr in a scheme to create their own empire in

the West. Burr and Dayton were arrested and charged with treason. Burr was acquitted, and charges against Dayton were dropped, but there are strong indications that both men were involved in a treasonous plot.

Although Jonathan Dayton's career in national politics was over, he was elected to the New Jersey legislature, where he served in 1814–15. The youngest Founding Father, whose life had gone downhill after he performed the greatest act of his life, died in Elizabeth, New Jersey, on October 9, 1824, a week before what would have been his sixty-fourth birthday.

IV. GEORGIA

Spain built a fort in Georgia in 1566 and some missions there soon after. Spanish efforts to rule the region failed, however, and Georgia wasn't colonized until the 1700s, when Englishman James Oglethorpe decided to establish a haven for debtors and other poor people. King George II granted permission, and the colony was named Georgia in his honor.

Oglethorpe and approximately 120 settlers sailed for America in late 1732. In February 1733 they founded Savannah, Georgia's first European-built town. Georgia was the last of England's thirteen American colonies to be permanently settled.

At first James Oglethorpe made certain that Georgia had no slavery. But in 1750, after the "Father of Georgia" had returned to England, the ban on slavery was ended. White Georgians then imported slaves to grow their rice, corn, and other crops.

By 1787 Georgia was home to 75,000 people, nearly 30,000 of them slaves. Although Georgia ranked ahead of only Delaware and Rhode Island in population, its leaders expected that Georgia would one day be very populous. As a result, Georgia's delegates often sided with the large states at the Constitutional Convention. Georgia became our fourth state by approving the Constitution on January 2, 1788.

Georgia, which was nicknamed the Peach State because it produced so much of that fruit, fulfilled expectations. By the year 2000 it ranked tenth among the fifty states in population. Because of its booming population and diverse industries, Georgia in recent times has become known as the Empire State of the South. Atlanta has been Georgia's state capital since 1868.

GEORGIA

Name	Birth Date	Age at Signing	Marriage(s)	Children	Death Date	Age at Death
ABRAHAM BALDWIN	November 22, 1754	32	Didn't marry	0	March 4, 1807	52
WILLIAM FEW	June 8, 1748	39	Catherine Nicholson	3	July 16, 1828	80

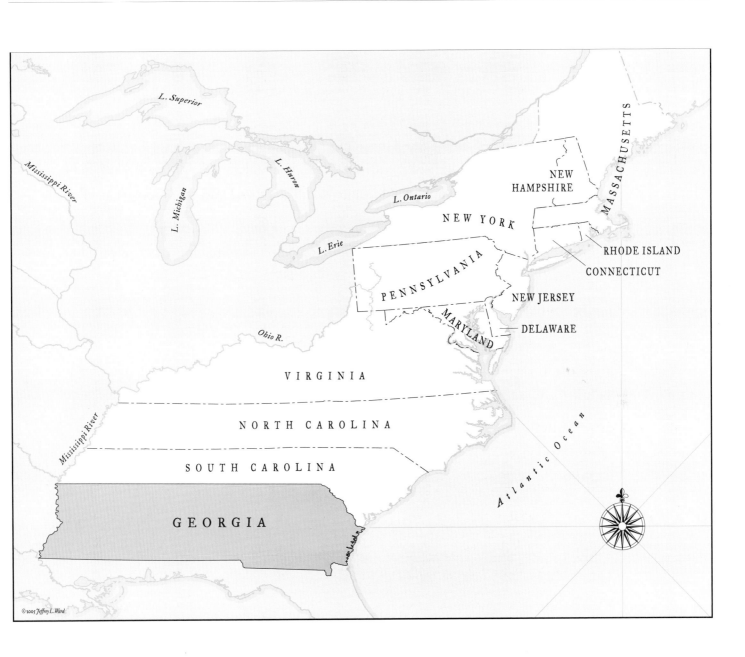

© 2005 Jeffrey L. Ward

ABRAHAM BALDWIN
His Vote Saved the Convention

Abr Baldwin

ONE OF TWELVE CHILDREN, Abraham Baldwin was born in North Guilford, Connecticut, on November 22, 1754. His father, a blacksmith, was determined to provide his children with a good education. When Abraham was only thirteen, his father enrolled him at Yale College in nearby New Haven, Connecticut. Abraham graduated four years later, then studied to become a minister. He received a clergyman's license in 1775, but instead of finding a position in a church, he stayed on at Yale for another four years to work as a tutor.

By then the Revolutionary War was raging. In 1779 Baldwin resigned his tutorial position to join the Continental Army as a chaplain. He suffered through the terrible winter of 1779–80 in Morristown, New Jersey, ministering to George Washington's 12,000 men.

At the end of the war Baldwin gave up the ministry, studied law, and became an attorney in Fairfield, Connecticut. In 1784 he moved to Georgia, settling in the Augusta region. Within a year he had begun practicing law and had been elected to Georgia's legislature, where he worked to improve the state's schools. He helped establish a state educational system for Georgia, and in 1785 he was instrumental in founding Georgia's first college, the University of Georgia.

Also in 1785, Baldwin was chosen to represent Georgia in the Continental Congress. He headed the Georgia delegation for the next three years. Then in 1787 he was appointed to represent Georgia at the Constitutional Convention, where he cast a crucial vote.

On July 2 the delegates voted on the most controversial issue they faced: Should all the states have an equal number of U.S. senators, regardless of population? Eleven states were represented at the convention at the time, for New Hampshire's delegates hadn't yet arrived, and Rhode Island never sent any.

Five states—Connecticut, New York, New Jersey, Delaware, and Maryland—favored equal representation in the Senate. Five others—Virginia, Pennsylvania, North Carolina, South Carolina, and Massachusetts—wanted the big states to have more senators. Georgia, the last state to vote on the issue, would decide the outcome.

William Houstoun and Abraham Baldwin were the only two Georgians present. Houstoun voted for the big states to have more senators. Baldwin was expected to do the same, but he knew that if they didn't have equal representation in the Senate, the small-state delegates might walk out, ending the proceedings. To keep things going, Baldwin switched his vote and went along with the small states. The result was a stalemate—five states in favor of equal representation in the

Senate, five opposed, with Georgia split. Baldwin's vote had kept the convention from coming to a premature close. A committee that was appointed to deliberate the matter then approved the Connecticut Compromise, which called for equal representation in the Senate.

The year Baldwin helped create the Constitution—1787—his father died. The blacksmith had fallen into debt trying to educate his children. Abraham, who never married, paid off his father's debts and finished educating his sisters and brothers out of his own pocket.

Abraham Baldwin served Georgia for the rest of his life. He was elected to the first House of Representatives under the new constitution, holding a seat for a decade (1789–99). Next Baldwin was elected to the Senate, where he served for eight years (1799–1807). The man who had saved the Constitutional Convention was in the midst of his second senatorial term when he died in Washington, D.C., on March 4, 1807, at the age of fifty-two. Baldwin County, Georgia, and Baldwin County, Alabama, were both named in honor of the founder of the University of Georgia.

WILLIAM FEW
"The Spirit of an American"

William Few [signature]

WILLIAM FEW WAS BORN near Baltimore, Maryland, on June 8, 1748. At about the age of seven, he was sent to a school near his home. Few later described his miserable experience at this country school:

> The teacher was an ill-natured man, who punished with rigor, and enforced his [rules] by terror. I detested the man, the school, and the books, and spent six or eight months at that school in terror and anxiety, with very little benefit.

Nonetheless, William was eager to learn. He studied on his own, even stealing glances at books in the midst of his farm chores.

In 1758, ten-year-old William moved with his family to North Carolina. Settling in Orange County along the frontier, the Fews became involved in the Regulator movement. The Regulators were frontiersmen who, feeling that they didn't have enough say in running North Carolina, revolted against the colonial government in the early 1770s. One of William's brothers was hanged for taking part in the Regulator revolt, and the British destroyed the Fews' farm.

Except for William, who remained behind in North Carolina for several years to wrap up his family's affairs, the Fews then moved on to Georgia. In his spare time William studied law—again on his own. The year independence was declared—1776—William joined his family in the Augusta, Georgia, area. He had learned so much by reading law books that he was admitted to be an attorney and began practicing in Augusta.

His family's experience in the Regulator revolt had made William violently anti-British. Possessing "the spirit of an American," as he later explained, he joined a militia unit that opposed the British in Georgia and Florida during the Revolutionary War. He also entered politics. In 1777 the self-taught lawyer was elected to serve at the convention that created a Georgia state constitution and also to the new state legislature. Three years later he was elected to the Continental Congress, where he represented Georgia from 1780 to 1789.

Because New York was the young country's capital between 1785 and 1790, Few spent much of his time in that city. While in New York he met Catherine Nicholson, whom he married in about 1786. The couple had three children, all girls.

In 1787 Few was elected to represent Georgia at the Constitutional Convention. He made no speeches, but signed the document and took part in the convention that made Georgia the fourth state on January 2, 1788. Few was then elected to serve as one of Georgia's two original U.S. senators. He held a Senate seat from 1789 to 1793 and followed that by serving in the Georgia legislature and as a judge.

Catherine apparently became homesick for New York, while William grew to dislike what he termed "the scorching climate of Georgia" and "the evils of Negro slavery." William, Catherine, and their children moved to New York City in 1799. Although New York allowed slavery, too, it wasn't nearly as extensive as in Georgia.

Few quickly made himself at home in his new state, serving in New York's legislature from 1802 to 1805. Among his later positions, he was president of the City Bank of New York and of the New York Eye Infirmary. He was greatly pleased when New York outlawed slavery in 1827. The next year, on July 16, 1828, eighty-year-old William Few died at his daughter's home in what is now Beacon, New York.

V. CONNECTICUT

In 1614 Adriaen Block of the Netherlands became the first European to explore Connecticut. During the 1630s English people from Massachusetts founded the region's first permanent colonial towns, including Windsor, Wethersfield, Hartford, and New Haven. A river the Indians called Quinnehtukqut flowed through the area. The English retained this Indian name, which means "Long River," and also gave it to the colony. However, they changed the spelling to *Connecticut*.

Connecticut colonists grew wheat, apples, and corn. The colony was also an early industrial center. Its people made many items, including hats, tinware, nails, clocks, and silk cloth. Salesmen known as "Yankee peddlers" traveled around selling Connecticut-made goods. There are various ideas as to how the word *Yankee* originated, but in any case the word became a nickname for people from the northern states and eventually for all Americans.

With 230,000 people, Connecticut was tied with South Carolina as the seventh-most-populous state as of 1787. Fittingly, the delegates from this middle-sized state helped solve the dispute between the large and small states by offering the Connecticut Compromise at the Constitutional Convention. Connecticut ratified the Constitution on January 9, 1788, entering the Union as the fifth state. Nearly a century later, in 1875, Hartford became Connecticut's permanent capital. Partly because the Connecticut Compromise meant so much to our national governmental framework and partly because of an early constitution it enacted in colonial days, Connecticut is nicknamed the Constitution State.

CONNECTICUT

Name	Birth Date	Age at Signing	Marriage(s)	Children	Death Date	Age at Death
ROGER SHERMAN*	April 19, 1721	66	Elizabeth Hartwell Rebecca Prescott	15	July 23, 1793	72
WILLIAM SAMUEL JOHNSON	October 7, 1727	59	Ann Beach Mary Beach	11	November 14, 1819	92

An asterisk (*) after a founder's name indicates that he also signed the Declaration of Independence.

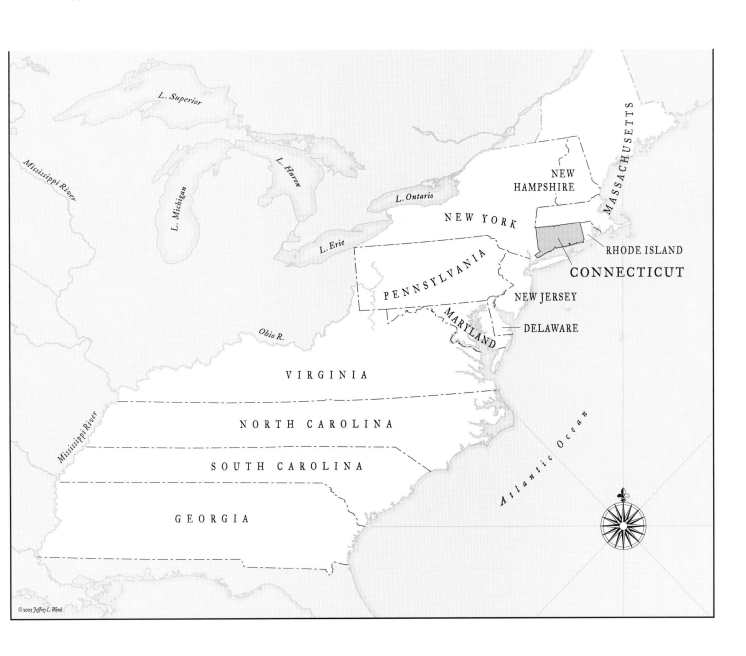

ROGER SHERMAN
"A Solid, Sensible Man"

Roger Sherman

ROGER SHERMAN WAS BORN on April 19, 1721 in Newton, Massachusetts, outside Boston. At the age of two he moved with his family to what is now Canton, Massachusetts, also near Boston. As a child, Roger worked on his family's farm and assisted his father, who was a shoemaker. While attending local schools, Roger delved into such subjects as mathematics, astronomy, and history. According to tradition, his love for study was so great that he kept an open book on his cobbler's bench so that he could read while he made shoes.

In 1741, Roger's father died. Two years later, the Shermans moved to New Milford, Connecticut, where Roger's older brother William had previously settled. It was said that twenty-two-year-old Roger Sherman made the nearly 150-mile journey on foot, carrying his shoemaker's tools on his back.

Once settled in New Milford, Sherman didn't make shoes for long. His mathematical ability helped him become a surveyor. He also bought land, and was soon one of New Milford's most prosperous citizens. With his brother William, Roger ran a country store. In his spare time he read law books, and at the age of thirty-two he became an attorney. Although Ben Franklin's *Poor Richard's Almanac* sold many more copies, Sherman also published his own almanac between 1750 and 1761. Very popular in the 1700s, almanacs were booklets that contained calendars, weather forecasts, and astronomical predictions, plus assorted facts and witty sayings.

Meanwhile, Sherman was raising a large family. In 1749 he had married his hometown sweetheart from Massachusetts, Elizabeth Hartwell. During their eleven years of marriage, Roger and Elizabeth had seven children. Elizabeth died in 1760 at the age of only thirty-four. Three years later Roger married Rebecca Prescott, with whom he had eight more children.

Perhaps being the father of fifteen children prepared Sherman for the career that became his life's work: politics. He began in New Milford, where he held such positions as assistant town clerk, fence viewer, and a town official called a selectman. In 1755 he was elected to the Connecticut legislature, and he also was a judge for many years. After moving to New Haven, Connecticut, in 1761, Sherman served as the treasurer of Yale College and as mayor of the city.

In 1774 Sherman was sent to represent Connecticut at the Continental Congress, starting a nearly twenty-year period as a national politician. He became known among his colleagues for his sound judgment and ability to work out problems. His fellow congressman John Adams called Sherman "a solid, sensible man" and added that he was "honest as an angel, and firm in the cause of American in-

dependence." Sherman was on the committee asked to draft the Declaration of Independence. Although Thomas Jefferson did almost all of the writing, some of Sherman's ideas went into the Declaration, which he signed.

His greatest achievement came eleven years later at the Constitutional Convention, where he was Mr. Compromise. For example, at first Sherman wanted to revise the Articles of Confederation, yet he agreed to the creation of a new framework of government when he saw how the majority felt. He preferred that the national legislature elect the president, but gave way to the more popular idea of having the people elect the president through the Electoral College.

The ex-shoemaker was mainly responsible for the compromise that saved the convention. As the meeting reached what Sherman called a "full stop" over the issue of representation in the legislature, he pushed through the Connecticut Compromise—the arrangement by which each state has two senators but a number of House members based on population. What few people realize today is that Sherman personally preferred a one-house legislature over a Congress composed of two houses!

At sixty-six, Sherman was the Constitution's oldest signer except for Ben Franklin. After the signing, he wrote a series of newspaper articles that helped win Connecticut's ratification on January 9, 1788. The architect of the Connecticut Compromise served in both houses of the U.S. legislature in his last years. From 1789 to 1791 he represented the Constitution State in the House of Representatives. He then served in the U.S. Senate from 1791 until his death in New Haven on July 23, 1793, at the age of seventy-two.

WILLIAM SAMUEL JOHNSON
"One Grand System"

WILLIAM SAMUEL JOHNSON WAS BORN in Stratford, Connecticut, on October 7, 1727. His father, a minister, taught "Sammy" at home, enabling him to enter Connecticut's Yale College when he was not quite thirteen. Sammy graduated in 1744 at sixteen.

The year of his graduation, England and France began one of their periodic wars for control of North America. Sammy's dream was to become a soldier for Britain, but his father wanted him to become a clergyman like himself. As a compromise, they agreed on a law career for Sammy. He studied law at home, and in 1749 became a practicing attorney. That year he married Ann Beach. The couple had eleven children, only four of whom survived childhood.

When America was young, families were often related in multiple ways. This was because towns were small, travel was difficult, and there wasn't a large pool from which to choose a spouse. Several years after he married Ann, William Samuel Johnson's mother died. His father then married Ann's mother, making her both William Samuel's mother-in-law and his stepmother.

Johnson became a successful attorney, attracting clients from his own colony as well as New York. In fact, it was said that he was the first person in Connecticut to earn his living solely by practicing law. Then in 1765 he was elected to the Connecticut legislature, beginning a long career in public office.

From 1767 to 1771 Johnson was in England representing Connecticut on colonial business. Observing events in England firsthand, Johnson became convinced that the problems resulted from a lack of communication rather than a British plot to oppress Americans.

When war broke out, Johnson retired from politics rather than choose either side. "I could not join in war against England and much less against my own country," he explained. Other Connecticut leaders were enraged at him for not supporting America, and in 1779 he was arrested and nearly imprisoned. Only after he took an oath of loyalty to Connecticut and convinced Governor Jonathan Trumbull that he was not on the British side was he released.

Even his enemies admired Johnson for doing what he felt was right regardless of the consequences. He regained his popularity at the end of the war and in 1784 was elected to the Continental Congress. Three years later he was chosen as one of Connecticut's delegates to the Constitutional Convention.

In Philadelphia, Johnson repeatedly reminded his colleagues that they must iron out their differences. He helped present the Connecticut Compromise, making a speech in which he said that "in one branch [the House of Representatives] the people ought to be represented, and in the other [the Senate] the states."

After signing the Constitution, Johnson spoke in support of the document at Connecticut's ratification convention:

> Our commerce is annihilated. Our national honor is no more. We have got to the very brink of ruin. We must adopt ... one grand system. If we reject [this] plan of government, I fear our national existence must come to a final end.

Later in life, Johnson served as a U.S. senator and as president of what is now Columbia University in New York City. His wife, Ann, died in 1796 after nearly fifty years of marriage. Five years later, toward the end of 1801, seventy-four-year-old William Samuel Johnson married Mary Beach, the widow of Ann's brother. This meant that Mary Beach, Johnson's sister-in-law, was now also his wife. Johnson lived to an older age than any other signer of the Constitution. He died on November 14, 1819, a month past his ninety-second birthday.

VI. MASSACHUSETTS

The settlement of Massachusetts began when English people known as Pilgrims founded Plymouth in 1620, allegedly stepping on Plymouth Rock as they came ashore. A decade later, in 1630, Boston was established. The capital of Massachusetts since the year of its founding, Boston became one of the great cities of the thirteen colonies.

Massachusetts contributed more to education than any other American colony. America's first college, Harvard, was founded at Cambridge in 1636. Also in Cambridge, father and son Stephen and Matthew Daye produced the first English-language book published in America in 1640. In 1647 Massachusetts passed a law requiring each town with fifty or more families to maintain a school partly supported by taxes. This marked the start of America's public school system. America's first successful newspaper, the *Boston News-Letter*, began publication in 1704.

During the Revolutionary era, Massachusetts was the most rebellious colony. The Boston Massacre and the Boston Tea Party helped spark the conflict with England. The war for independence began in 1775 when American patriots fought English troops at Lexington and Concord, Massachusetts.

With 350,000 people, Massachusetts was the fourth-most-populous colony by 1787. Many Massachusetts citizens agreed with one of their Constitutional Convention delegates, Elbridge Gerry, who refused to sign the document. Distrust of a strong central government was a main reason for opposition to the Constitution in Massachusetts. Only after a hotly contested struggle did the Bay State approve the Constitution on February 6, 1788, thereby becoming state number six.

MASSACHUSETTS

Name	Birth Date	Age at Signing	Marriage(s)	Children	Death Date	Age at Death
NATHANIEL GORHAM	May 27, 1738	49	Rebecca Call	9	June 11, 1796	58
RUFUS KING	March 24, 1755	32	Mary Alsop	7	April 29, 1827	72

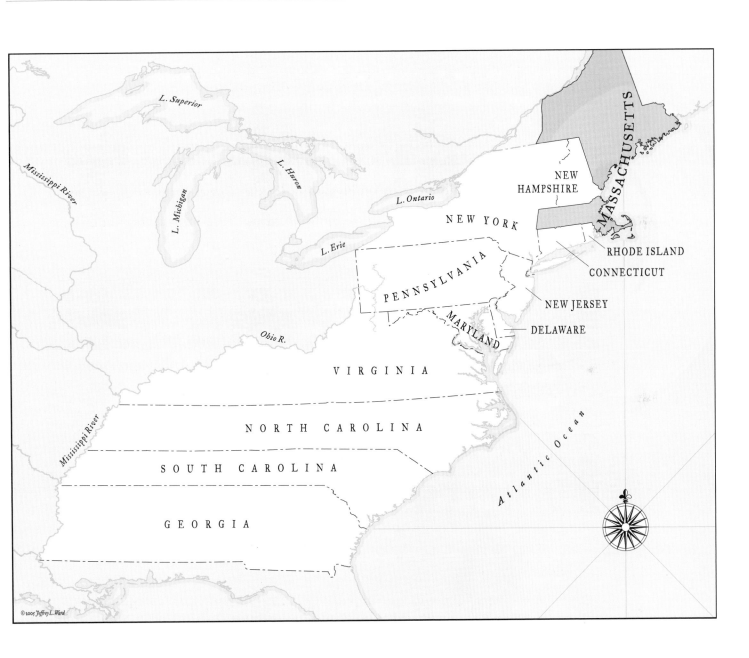

NATHANIEL GORHAM

"High in Reputation, and Much in the Esteem of His Countrymen"

Nathaniel Gorham

NATHANIEL GORHAM WAS BORN on May 27, 1738, in Charlestown, which today is part of Boston. At fifteen he was apprenticed to a merchant in New London, Connecticut. In exchange for food and a place to sleep, Nathaniel worked for the merchant for six years, until he was twenty-one. His master taught him well, for Nathaniel returned to Charlestown, opened his own merchant business, and was on the path to wealth by his mid-twenties. In 1763, the twenty-five-year-old businessman married Rebecca Call, with whom he had five daughters and four sons.

Gorham became involved in politics during the Revolutionary era. For many years he held a seat in the Massachusetts legislature, and from 1778 to 1781 he served as a member of the Massachusetts Board of War.

Massachusetts sent Gorham to serve in the Continental Congress for several years in the 1780s. Likable, a fine speaker, and an outstanding organizer, Gorham was elected president of Congress on June 6, 1786. He was president when Shays's Rebellion took place in 1786–87. Convinced that only a very powerful leader could hold the new nation together, Gorham wrote to Prince Henry of Prussia (a German kingdom), asking him to consider becoming king of the United States. Fortunately, few people besides Nathaniel Gorham took his proposal seriously.

Gorham was selected as a delegate to the Constitutional Convention, where he impressed his colleagues as a natural leader. William Pierce wrote of him, "Mr. Gorham is a merchant in Boston, high in reputation, and much in the esteem of his countrymen. He is a Man of very good sense."

His fellow delegates elected Nathaniel Gorham to an important position:

president of the Committee of the Whole, which was composed of all the delegates at the convention. The purpose of this committee was to allow the delegates to speak more informally than they did during the official proceedings. Whenever the delegates wanted to transform themselves into the Committee of the Whole, convention president George Washington left his chair and was replaced by Gorham. Once the Committee of the Whole completed its session, Washington returned to his chair, and the convention continued.

Gorham favored a strong federal government and argued for granting the president broad powers. He also suggested a last-second change in the Constitution. In Article I, Section II, it had been agreed that there would be one member of the House of Representatives "for every forty Thousand inhabitants." Just before the Constitution was to be signed, Gorham asked that the number be reduced to thirty thousand so that there would be more representatives.

At that late date his proposal probably would have been voted down, if not for one thing. George Washington, offering an opinion for the only time at the convention, said that he agreed with Mr. Gorham. The proposal passed unanimously. Later, the nation grew too populous to maintain one representative for every 30,000 Americans. In 1929, Congress decided to limit the House to 435 members, which now averages out to one representative for every 700,000 Americans.

Back in Massachusetts, Gorham took part in the convention that adopted the Constitution by a close vote on February 6, 1788. He then retired from politics. Late in life, Gorham became involved in land deals that went sour, and suffered bankruptcy. Nathaniel Gorham, who had helped run the Constitutional Convention, died of a stroke on June 11, 1796, at the age of fifty-eight.

RUFUS KING
He Fought Slavery

Rufus King

RUFUS KING WAS BORN in Scarborough, Maine, on March 24, 1755. At that time, Maine was part of the Massachusetts Colony. In fact, not until it became a state in 1820 did Maine separate from Massachusetts.

For about four years Rufus attended a grammar school in Scarborough before heading off to an academy in Massachusetts to prepare for college. He studied at the academy for six years, then entered Harvard at eighteen. After graduating in 1777, he moved to Newburyport, Massachusetts, to study law. He wanted to help his country win its independence, though, so the next year he became an aide to General John Glover during the campaign to seize Newport, Rhode Island, from the British. One morning Major King was eating breakfast at Glover's headquarters when the general ordered him to investigate nearby cannon fire. As soon as King left the table, another officer, Henry Sherburne, took his empty seat. Suddenly a cannonball burst through the window, shattering Sherburne's leg. Whenever King saw Sherburne hobbling around on his wooden leg after that, he commented, "By right I should be wearing it."

The attempt to take Newport failed, and after a few weeks King gave up the military life and resumed his law studies. He was admitted to the bar in 1780 and opened his law office in Newburyport. An outstanding lawyer and speaker, King was elected to the Massachusetts legislature in 1783 and to the Continental Congress the following year.

Massachusetts had become the first of the original thirteen colonies to outlaw slavery in 1780. Like many other northerners, King hated slavery. On March 16, 1785, he introduced a measure in Congress that would ban slavery in new states carved out of the Northwest Territory, a vast region claimed by the United

States. Two years later Congress finally passed an antislavery ordinance based on King's proposal.

Also in 1787 the Massachusetts legislature chose King to attend the convention in Philadelphia. Just thirty-two years old, he was one of the youngest delegates. At first he opposed a major overhaul of the Articles of Confederation, but he quickly did an about-face, becoming one of the convention's most eloquent spokesmen for a strong central government. In early August he made an impassioned speech condemning the importation of slaves into the United States. Although the southern states wouldn't agree to immediately stop bringing slaves into the country, King helped push through a clause in Article I, Section 9, that opened the possibility of ending the slave trade in 1808. Serving as a delegate to his state's ratification convention a few months after he signed the document, King helped win approval of the Constitution.

Rufus King had married Mary Alsop, the sixteen-year-old daughter of a New York merchant, in 1786. By 1788 the couple had settled in New York City. Mary and Rufus King had seven children—six sons and a daughter.

King continued his political career in his new home. In 1789 he was elected U.S. senator for the Empire State. In 1816 he ran for president, but lost to James Monroe. Later, in the Senate, King became an even more determined foe of slavery. In February 1820 he made a Senate speech in which he declared that slavery violated the principles of freedom for which America stood:

> I have yet to learn that one man can make a slave of another. I hold that all laws imposing any such condition upon any human being are absolutely void, because [they are] contrary to the law of God.

After a lifetime of public service, Rufus King died in New York City on April 29, 1827, at the age of seventy-two.

VII. MARYLAND

Englishman John Smith, a leader of the Virginia Colony, explored Maryland in 1608. Largely due to the efforts of the Calvert family, permanent English settlement began in the 1630s. England's King Charles I granted the Calverts a large tract of land and named the region Terra Maria (Latin, meaning "Land of Maria") for his wife, Queen Henrietta Maria. Later the name was translated into English as Maryland.

The Calverts, who were known as the Lords Baltimore, established Maryland as a colony where Catholics and members of other persecuted faiths were welcome. The city of Baltimore was named in their honor, as were the songbirds called Baltimore orioles.

Although Marylanders grew corn, wheat, and other food crops, tobacco soon became the colony's leading crop. Tobacco was even used as money by Marylanders, who paid rents, debts, and taxes with it.

By the time of the Constitutional Convention, Maryland was home to three hundred thousand people, a third of whom were slaves. Maryland was tied with New York as the fifth-most-populous state. Maryland became our seventh state under the Constitution by ratifying the document on April 28, 1788.

George Washington gave Maryland its nickname by praising its "troops of the line," or Revolutionary War soldiers, for their bravery in fighting the British. Because of that, Maryland became known as the Old Line State. Annapolis has been Maryland's capital since 1694. Washington, D.C., which has been our permanent national capital since 1800, is composed of land that was once part of Maryland.

MARYLAND

Name	Birth Date	Age at Signing	Marriage(s)	Children	Death Date	Age at Death
James McHenry	November 16, 1753	33	Peggy Caldwell	5	May 3, 1816	62
Daniel of St. Thomas Jenifer	1723	64	Didn't marry	0	November 16, 1790	67
Daniel Carroll	July 22, 1730	57	Eleanor Carroll	2	May 7, 1796	65

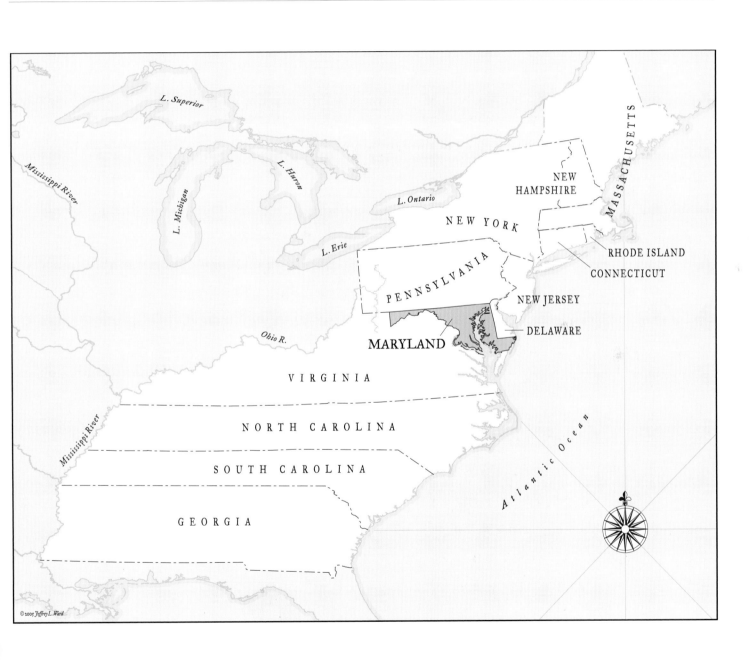

JAMES McHENRY
"All the Support in My Power"

James McHenry

JAMES McHENRY WAS BORN in what is now Northern Ireland on November 16, 1753. It was said that while attending an academy in Dublin, Ireland, he made himself ill by studying too much. In 1771 his family sent the seventeen-year-old James to recuperate in America, arranging for him to live in Philadelphia with a baker. This man had a nine-year-old stepdaughter named Margaret Caldwell, who was nicknamed Peggy. While recovering his health, James taught Peggy how to read and write.

Meanwhile, James was sending glowing descriptions of America to his family. In 1772 his parents and younger brother followed him to the new country. His father and brother established a store in Baltimore that made the McHenry family wealthy.

The year of his family's arrival, James was sent to attend Newark Academy in Delaware. While there, he discovered that he loved to write poems. During his life McHenry wrote hundreds of poems. He wrote poems to his friends, love poems to young ladies, and poems to celebrate happy occasions. Although none of his poems were published, he greatly enjoyed creating them.

James McHenry remained at Newark Academy a short time, then returned to Philadelphia to study medicine under noted physician Benjamin Rush. The Revolution broke out around the time that McHenry completed his medical training. "Mac," as his friends called him, wanted to help his adopted country win independence. During the war he served as an army surgeon and as an aide to General Washington and to the Marquis de Lafayette, a French soldier fighting on the American side.

By the war's end, McHenry had moved to Baltimore, Maryland, where his parents and brother had settled. In early 1784 he married Peggy Caldwell, whom he had taught to read and write when she was a child. James and Peggy McHenry had five children—three daughters and two sons. An affectionate and loving husband, McHenry wrote poems to his wife whenever they were apart.

Following the Revolution, McHenry gave up medicine. He had become more interested in politics. In 1781 he was elected to the Maryland senate, and two years later he was sent to represent Maryland in the Continental Congress. For a while he served in Maryland's senate and in Congress at the same time.

In the spring of 1787 the Maryland legislature appointed McHenry to attend the Constitutional Convention. He said little at the gathering in Philadelphia,

but kept notes that have provided us with insight into the discussions. He explained in his notebook why he finally decided to sign the Constitution despite his misgivings about a strong central government:

> Comparing the inconveniences and the evils which we labor under from the present confederation with the probable benefits promised us by the new system, I am clear that I ought to give it all the support in my power.
>
> Philada. 17 Sept. 1787. James McHenry

As he had written in his notebook, McHenry supported the Constitution at Maryland's ratifying convention. His efforts helped Maryland become the seventh state when it approved the Constitution on April 28, 1788.

For several years McHenry served in the legislature of the Old Line State. Among other things, he worked for the gradual freeing of slaves. Then in January 1796, the nation's first president, George Washington, sent his old Revolutionary War aide a letter saying, "It would give me sincere pleasure if you will fill the office of Secretary of War."

McHenry accepted, and held the post of secretary of war for four years. He helped organize the army and establish regulations for the military, but he was too gentle a soul to run the war department effectively. In May 1800 he was dismissed from the post by the second president, John Adams. McHenry retired to spend his time with his family and write his poems. Revolutionary War surgeon, aide to General Washington, Founding Father, secretary of war, and poet, James McHenry died at his home near Baltimore on May 3, 1816, at the age of sixty-two. Baltimore's Fort McHenry, where the flag flew that inspired Francis Scott Key to compose "The Star-Spangled Banner" in 1814, was named for James McHenry.

DANIEL OF
ST. THOMAS JENIFER
The "Good Humour" Man

DANIEL OF ST. THOMAS JENIFER WAS BORN in Maryland's Charles County sometime in 1723. He was of English ancestry on his father's side and of Swedish heritage on his mother's side. There are several theories about how Daniel received his odd middle name, which is sometimes spelled out "of Saint Thomas." According to one story, the name honored an earlier family member who had visited the island of St. Thomas in the Virgin Islands before settling in Maryland.

Daniel was educated at home by tutors. While still a youth, he helped manage the family property, which included extensive lands as well as slaves. At the age of only twenty-six, he became a justice of the peace in his native Charles County. Then in the 1750s he represented his county in Maryland's colonial legislature. A few years later, he helped settle a long-standing dispute between Maryland and Pennsylvania over their border. In 1760 Jenifer was named to a commission that was asked to solve the disagreement. The commission hired two Englishmen, Charles Mason and Jeremiah Dixon, to survey the border between the two colonies. Mason and Dixon finished their survey in 1767. Their famous Mason-Dixon line not only determined the boundary between Pennsylvania and Maryland but also became known as the line that separates the North from the South.

Jenifer became a leader in Maryland's revolutionary government during the struggle with England. From 1775 to 1777 he was president of Maryland's Council of Safety, which organized the fight against British rule. In the late 1770s and early 1780s he served in the Maryland senate while finding time to represent his state in the Continental Congress.

In 1785 delegates from Maryland and Virginia met at Mount Vernon, the Virginia home of George Washington, to discuss matters of mutual interest to the two states. Jenifer represented Maryland at this Mount Vernon conference. It led to the better-known Annapolis Convention the following year, which in turn resulted in the Constitutional Convention the year after that.

Jenifer wasn't selected as one of Maryland's original delegates to the Philadelphia convention, but was added later as a replacement for a man who couldn't go. He arrived eight days after the convention opened but then attended nearly every session to the end. His fellow delegates found him to be a quiet, good-natured man. Jenifer "is always in good humour, and never fails to make his company pleased with him," wrote William Pierce.

Jenifer took only one important stand at the convention, arguing for a three- instead of a two-year term in the House of Representatives, because the best politicians would not seek a position they might soon lose. He lost that point, but to this day many people believe that the two-year term for representatives is too short. At sixty-four, Jenifer was the third-oldest signer of the Constitution, behind only Benjamin Franklin and Roger Sherman.

Daniel of St. Thomas Jenifer, who never married, enjoyed exchanging visits with friends such as George Washington in his later years. On November 16, 1790, Jenifer died in Annapolis, Maryland, at the age of sixty-seven. In his will he ordered that the slaves he owned be freed six years after his death.

DANIEL CARROLL
He Helped Write the First Amendment

Dan⟨l⟩ Carroll

DANIEL CARROLL WAS BORN in the town of Upper Marlboro, Maryland, on July 22, 1730. He was of Irish Catholic descent. Religious prejudice was common in colonial America when Daniel was growing up. Catholics, Jewish people, and members of other religious minorities were often persecuted because of their faith. Maryland had laws preventing Catholics from voting, holding public office, or building their own churches. Because of another law forbidding the establishment of Catholic schools, Daniel was tutored at home. At the age of twelve he was sent to France, where he attended school for six years.

By the time he returned home to Maryland, Daniel was eighteen. Four years later he married Eleanor Carroll, who was his cousin. Daniel and Eleanor had two children—a son and a daughter. During the 1750s and 1760s, Daniel Carroll enjoyed the life of a prosperous tobacco planter. He eventually accumulated 7,800 acres of land (more than twelve square miles) and at least thirty-two slaves.

In 1776 Maryland adopted its first state constitution, which granted Catholics the right to vote and hold office. Almost immediately Daniel Carroll entered public service, where he would remain for the rest of his life. He began by serving in Maryland's revolutionary government from 1777 to 1781. He was then elected to the Continental Congress, where he signed the Articles of Confederation.

Daniel Carroll had a famous brother, John Carroll, who was the first Catholic bishop in the United States. Daniel also had an illustrious cousin, Charles Carroll of Carrollton, who signed the Declaration of Independence and who in 1787 was elected as one of Maryland's delegates to the Constitutional Convention. Charles Carroll of Carrollton declined to go, however, and his cousin Daniel was selected as a replacement. Daniel Carroll and Thomas FitzSimons of Pennsylvania were the only two Catholics to serve as delegates at the convention.

Arguing for a strong central government, Carroll spoke approximately twenty times at the convention. Back home, he wrote letters to newspapers praising the document he had helped create, using such pen names as "A Friend to the Constitution." His letter-writing campaign helped Maryland become the seventh state in the spring of 1788.

In 1789 Carroll was elected to the first U.S. House of Representatives, and served from that year until 1791. During his first year there, the U.S. Congress proposed a series of amendments to the Constitution designed to protect the rights of citizens. Ten of these were ratified, and in late 1791 they were added to the Constitution as the Bill of Rights. Daniel Carroll, who had suffered religious persecution, was partially responsible for the wording of the First Amendment, which among other things protected freedom of worship:

> *Amendment* 1: Congress shall make no law respecting an establishment of religion, or prohibiting the free exercise thereof; or abridging the freedom of speech, or of the press; or

the right of the people to peaceably assemble, and to petition the government for a redress of grievances.

Carroll also helped draft the Tenth Amendment, which assured the states and their citizens of retaining all their rights not granted to the federal government.

In January 1791 President Washington appointed Daniel Carroll as one of three commissioners in charge of surveying, designing, and building Washington, D.C. He held this position four years, helping to create the new permanent national capital. Due to poor health, he resigned the post in 1795. Daniel Carroll died at the age of sixty-five on May 7, 1796, in his home at Rock Creek, Maryland.

VIII. SOUTH CAROLINA

In 1526 Spaniards began a settlement along what is now the South Carolina coast. Had it lasted, it would have been the first permanent European colony in what is now the United States. However, due to hunger and other hardships the colony was soon abandoned.

English people named the region Carolana (Latin for "Land of Charles") in honor of England's King Charles I. Later the name was changed to Carolina, and the region was divided into North and South Carolina. In 1670 the first permanent colonial town in South Carolina was begun by the English. It was named Charleston in honor of England's King Charles II.

South Carolina settlers grew rice and indigo, a plant from which a blue dye was made. Some extremely wealthy planters built large plantations with lovely gardens and vast fields where slaves grew the crops. During the 1700s Charleston was the wealthiest town in England's thirteen American colonies.

By 1787 South Carolina was tied with Connecticut as the seventh-most-populous state. Of South Carolina's 230,000 people, about 105,000, or nearly half, were slaves. Expecting that South Carolina would one day be very populous (which never happened), its delegates often sided with the large states at the Constitutional Convention. On May 23, 1788, South Carolina became the eighth state to join the Union by approving the Constitution. Two years later in 1790 Columbia became the permanent capital of the Palmetto State, which earned its nickname at a Revolutionary War battle.

SOUTH CAROLINA

Name	Birth Date	Age at Signing	Marriage(s)	Children	Death Date	Age at Death
JOHN RUTLEDGE	1739, probably in September	48	Elizabeth Grimke	10	July 18, 1800	60
PIERCE BUTLER	July 11, 1744	43	Polly Middleton	8	February 15, 1822	77
CHARLES COTESWORTH PINCKNEY	February 25, 1746	41	Sally Middleton Mary Stead	4	August 16, 1825	79
CHARLES PINCKNEY	October 26, 1757	29	Polly Laurens	3	October 29, 1824	67

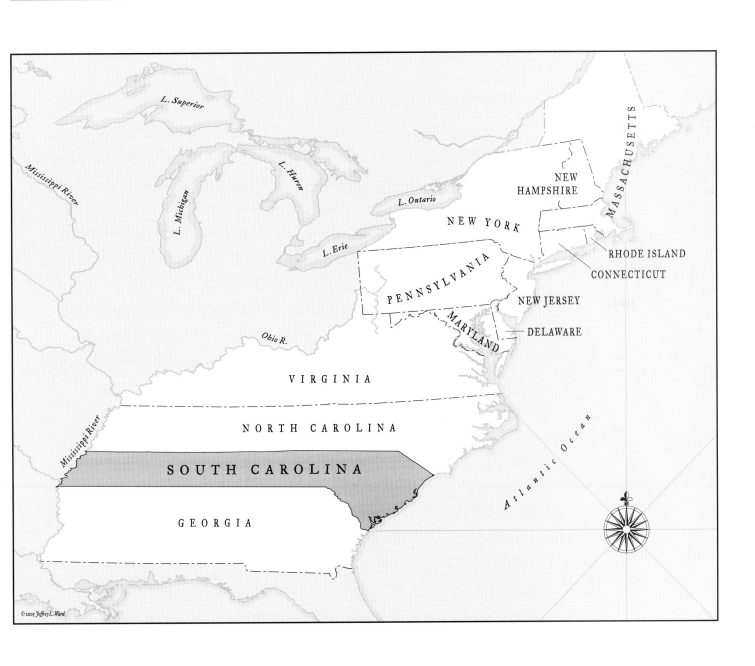

© 2005 Jeffrey L. Ward

JOHN RUTLEDGE
He Named His Son "States"

J. Rutledge

JOHN RUTLEDGE WAS BORN in 1739, probably in September, in or near Charleston, South Carolina. His father was a doctor. His mother, who was only fifteen years old at his birth, was said to be South Carolina's richest heiress.

John idolized his uncle Andrew Rutledge, who was a prominent attorney. Taught to read and write by tutors, John liked to "play lawyer" as a child. Pretending that his younger brothers and sister were the jurors, he would first argue one side of a case, then the other.

When John was eleven, his father died. He was ready to begin the serious study of law, John informed Andrew Rutledge. His uncle cleared a corner of his office, and there eleven-year-old John sat reading law books and helping with legal papers. A few years later he sailed to England to study law. By the age of twenty he had become an attorney and won several cases in England. He sailed home in late 1760, arriving in Charleston on Christmas Eve.

John Rutledge quickly became one of South Carolina's leading attorneys and politicians. In March 1761, at just twenty-one years of age, Rutledge was elected to the South Carolina colonial legislature. He married Elizabeth Grimke two years later. During their long and happy marriage, John and Elizabeth had ten children—seven boys and three girls.

Meanwhile, trouble between America and Britain was brewing. Having been educated in England, Rutledge had strong feelings of loyalty toward the mother country. But he eventually realized that the time had come for independence. In 1776 he helped write South Carolina's first state constitution and was elected as its first state governor.

Governor Rutledge took part in one of the most dramatic events of the Revolution. In mid-1776 a British fleet approached Charleston, intending to capture the city. As the enemy closed in, South Carolina's Colonel William Moultrie and his men were building Fort Sullivan to guard Charleston. The island where the fort stood contained many palmetto trees, so the patriots built the structure out of palmetto logs. The fort couldn't be defended and should be abandoned, American military leaders believed. Governor Rutledge disagreed vehemently, and sent this note to the fort:

To Colonel William Moultrie in chief command of Fort Sullivan

Sir:

General Lee still wishes you to evacuate the fort. You will not, without order from me. I would sooner cut off my hand than write one.

J. Rutledge

The Americans remained at the fort and fought the British fleet on June 28, 1776. The British, who had expected the fort to fall quickly under their bombard-

ment, were amazed to see their cannonballs sinking harmlessly into the soft palmetto logs. Thanks to the determination of Governor Rutledge, the bravery of Colonel Moultrie and his men, and the palmetto log fort, the Americans won the battle. Ever since, South Carolina has been known as the Palmetto State.

After the war, Rutledge served in the Continental Congress and as a judge. In 1787 he was selected to head the Palmetto State's four-man delegation to the Constitutional Convention, where he played a major role. He seconded the nomination of George Washington as convention president, and later chaired the Committee of Detail, which produced a rough draft of the Constitution. He also helped settle a controversial issue: how should power be divided between the federal government and the states?

Back in 1783 John and Elizabeth had named their tenth child States Rutledge as a living reminder that the United States was a union of states. At the convention, Rutledge argued that the states should decide certain matters for themselves, but in matters affecting the nation as a whole the federal government should reign supreme. He was largely responsible for the clause in Article VI declaring that "the laws of the United States . . . and all treaties made, or which shall be made, under the authority of the United States, shall be the supreme law of the land." Called the Linchpin of the Constitution, this section orders the states to obey laws and treaties made by the U.S. government even if they dislike them, and was a key factor in establishing the nation's stability.

Slavery was an issue that Rutledge felt each state should decide for itself. Due partly to his influence, nothing was placed in the Constitution to outlaw slavery, and Congress was forbidden from ending the importation of slaves until 1808. Ironically, Rutledge himself was becoming less involved in slaveowning. At the start of the Revolution he had owned about sixty slaves. By the time of the Constitutional Convention the number was reduced to twenty-eight, and at his death he would own just a single slave.

In 1791 John Rutledge became chief justice of the South Carolina Supreme Court. He was so depressed by his wife's death in 1792 that he lost his sanity at times. On one occasion he was prevented from drowning himself by a young slave girl's calls for help. John Rutledge died of natural causes on July 18, 1800, at the age of sixty.

PIERCE BUTLER
"I Shall Pray for Peace on Earth"

Pierce Butler [signature]

BORN IN IRELAND on July 11, 1744, Pierce Butler joined the British army when he was only eleven. Within three years he was a lieutenant serving in Canada during the French and Indian War, fought between Britain and France. In 1758 the fourteen-year-old officer was wounded helping British forces capture a French fort in Canada, but fortunately he recovered.

By 1766 Britain and the thirteen colonies were heading toward war. Now a twenty-two-year-old major, Butler was sent to the colonies to scout out places where British troops might be stationed. Butler fell in love with America—and with Mary Middleton, a wealthy young South Carolinian who was known as Polly. The couple married in early 1771. Butler then resigned from the army and settled down to the life of a rich South Carolina planter. With the help of hundreds of slaves, he grew cotton and rice on his plantations in South Carolina and Georgia. Pierce and Polly Butler had four daughters and four sons.

Although he had once fought for Britain, Butler sided with his adopted country in its war for independence. For a time, the Butler family had to flee South Carolina because the British occupied the state. When independence was finally won, Butler declared, "I have suffered so greatly by war that I shall the rest of my days pray for peace on Earth."

In 1776 Pierce Butler was elected to the South Carolina legislature, where he served many years. The South Carolina legislature chose Butler as one of its four delegates to the Constitutional Convention of 1787. He went to Philadelphia convinced that the country would collapse without a stronger central government.

Pierce Butler never hesitated to offer his opinions at the convention, speaking about seventy times. On the second day he suggested that the proceedings be kept secret. As of 1787 the country had approximately one hundred newspapers. If they were to report that the delegates were arguing over various issues, America would appear to be collapsing. Besides, if everyone knew what they were discussing, the delegates might be pressured to vote one way or another. His fellow delegates liked Butler's secrecy proposal and adopted it. Were it not for private notes made by James Madison, William Pierce, and James McHenry, we would know very little about the convention.

Butler was on the committee that created our system of electing the president—the Electoral College—which may have been his brainchild. According to Article II, Section I, of the Constitution, each state has a number of electors equal to the number of its senators and representatives in Congress. The candidate receiving the most popular votes from a state receives all of its electoral

votes, and the candidate with a majority of electoral votes becomes president. Since each state has two senators and at least one representative, even the least populous state has at least three electoral votes. The Electoral College enables the smaller states to have significant input in choosing the president, because their votes can mean the difference between a candidate winning or losing the nation's highest office.

Like other southern planters, Butler wanted the slave system to continue. He suggested what came to be known as the Constitution's fugitive slave clause, providing for the return of runaway slaves who cross state boundaries.

After signing the Constitution, Butler went back to South Carolina, where he won election as one of the Palmetto State's first two U.S. senators. He was later elected to two more Senate terms. Pierce Butler died on February 15, 1822, at the age of seventy-seven. Had he not been involved in the terrible institution of slavery, Butler might be remembered as one of the greatest of the Founding Fathers.

CHARLES COTESWORTH PINCKNEY

"My Heart Is Altogether American"

Charles Cotesworth Pinckney

ELIZABETH LUCAS WAS PROBABLY born on Antigua, a British-ruled island of the West Indies, where her father served in the English army. At fifteen, Eliza and her family moved to South Carolina, settling on a plantation near Charleston. When her father was recalled to Antigua, he placed sixteen-year-old Eliza in charge of his three South Carolina plantations. Besides managing the property, Eliza experimented with plants, including indigo, which was used to make a blue dye. Following several years of effort, Eliza grew a good indigo crop in 1744, when she was just twenty-one years old. Thanks to Eliza Lucas, indigo became an important crop in South Carolina.

Around the time of her triumph with indigo, Eliza married Charles Pinckney, a planter and lawyer. The oldest of the couple's four children, Charles Cotesworth Pinckney, was born in Charleston on February 25, 1746. Charles Cotesworth sailed to England with his family when he was seven. He spent the next sixteen years abroad, attending school in England and France and studying law in London. He returned to South Carolina in 1769 at the age of twenty-three, began practicing law, and in 1773 married Sarah Middleton, daughter of one of South Carolina's wealthiest citizens, Henry Middleton. Three daughters and a son were born to Charles Cotesworth and "Sally" Pinckney.

Although he had spent half his life in England and spoke and dressed like an English gentleman, Charles Cotesworth Pinckney sided with America in its struggle with the mother country. He headed the committee that created South Carolina's first state constitution in 1776. Pinckney also joined the American army as an aide to General Washington and fought in Pennsylvania, Georgia, and South Carolina. After the British captured Charleston in May 1780, Pinckney became a prisoner of war. The British tried to lure him to their side, but he defiantly responded, "My heart is altogether American, and neither severity nor favor nor poverty nor affluence can ever induce me to swerve from it." He was released in 1782, near the end of the war.

Five years later, Pinckney was chosen as a South Carolina delegate to the Constitutional Convention. One Pinckney suggestion that was adopted concerned freedom of religion. In colonial days, people of certain faiths had been prevented from holding office or voting. At Pinckney's insistence, a clause was inserted into Article VI stating that "no religious test shall ever be required as a qualification to any office or public trust under the United States."

Back home, Pinckney rallied support for the new constitution, helping to convince a convention meeting in Charleston to approve the document by a 149–73 vote on May 23, 1788. Two years later he took part in creating a new constitution for the Palmetto State. This made three constitutions he had helped

forge—the federal constitution as well as South Carolina's state constitutions of 1776 and 1790.

Meanwhile, in 1784, Sally Pinckney died of "consumption," as tuberculosis was then called. Two years later, Pinckney remarried. He and his second wife, Mary Stead Pinckney, didn't have any children together.

Later in life, Charles Cotesworth Pinckney ran unsuccessfully for the two highest offices in the land. In 1800 he ran for vice president but lost, and in 1804 and 1808 he ran for president but was defeated both times. The man who had helped create three constitutions died in Charleston on August 16, 1825 at the age of seventy-nine.

CHARLES PINCKNEY

"Equality Is the Leading Feature of the United States"

Charles Pinckney

CHARLES PINCKNEY WAS BORN in Charleston on October 26, 1757. He and Charles Cotesworth Pinckney were cousins. To add to the confusion over names in this famous family, the fathers of both cousins were also named Charles Pinckney!

Charles Pinckney the future Founding Father was brilliant from early youth. At fifteen, he was invited to attend law school in London, but because of the worsening relations with England he stayed home and studied in his father's law office in Charleston.

Following in the footsteps of other family members, Charles decided to enter politics. In November 1778, the young attorney ran for the South Carolina legislature. He later enjoyed telling a story about this first bid for elected office. The day of the election was so stormy that only two men dared come out to vote—Charles Pinckney and an employee of his father's. When the votes were tallied, twenty-one-year-old Charles Pinckney had won by a count of 2–0! He would serve his state and country in various ways over a period of more than forty years.

Pinckney fought in the Revolution and was captured when the British seized Charleston in May 1780. For a time he was held on a British prison ship, but in 1781 he was released.

After the war, Pinckney was elected to the Continental Congress, where he served from 1784 to 1787. In Congress he asserted that, to survive, the United States needed a much stronger government. Congress issued the call for a convention, and Charles Pinckney was chosen as a South Carolina delegate. At twenty-nine, Pinckney was one of the youngest delegates at the Constitutional Convention. He was also one of the most talkative, rising to speak more than a hundred times. According to James Madison, in one stirring speech Pinckney insisted that "a system must be suited to the people it is to govern," adding that

"Equality is the leading feature of the United States." This was a very democratic remark for the time, but, as the owner of 300 slaves, Pinckney was only talking about equality among *white* people.

Charles Pinckney presented what is sometimes called the Pinckney Plan to his fellow delegates. As a whole, it was not adopted by the convention. However, some scholars claim that more than thirty provisions in the finished Constitution were proposed by the young South Carolinian, including those creating a single leader called the president and a two-house Congress of the United States.

Back in South Carolina, Charles Pinckney launched the fight for ratification, which was accomplished in May 1788. That spring Charles Pinckney had another reason to celebrate. For two years he had been in love with Mary Eleanor Laurens, a South Carolina girl known as Polly. But Polly's father had decided that she was too young to marry and must wait until she was eighteen. The very day of her

eighteenth birthday, Polly and Charles Pinckney were married. The couple had three children—two daughters and a son.

In early 1789 Charles Pinckney was elected governor of South Carolina. He served as the Palmetto State's chief executive from that year until 1792, again from 1796 to 1798, and once more from 1806 to 1808. Among his other political offices, he represented the Palmetto State in the U.S. Senate from 1798 to 1801 and in the U.S. House of Representatives from 1819 to 1821.

The South Carolinian who had proposed many of the provisions that eventually became part of the Constitution died in Charleston on October 29, 1824, three days after his sixty-seventh birthday.

IX. NEW HAMPSHIRE

Martin Pring, an Englishman who arrived in 1603, was the first known explorer in this region. Twenty years later, New Hampshire, which was named for England's county of Hampshire, became the third of the thirteen colonies to be permanently settled. Only Virginia (1607) and Massachusetts (1620) came earlier. New Hampshire's first settlements were at Rye in 1623 and at Dover around the same time. Portsmouth was begun in 1631.

With its cold winters and rugged terrain, New Hampshire was a challenging place to live. Its people became known for their self-reliance and ability to make do with limited resources. New Hampshire families grew corn, beans, pumpkins, potatoes, and apples on their farms. In fact, potatoes didn't become an important food crop in America until Scotch-Irish settlers brought them when they founded Londonderry, New Hampshire in 1719.

New Hampshire had only 125,000 people by 1787; only Delaware, Rhode Island, and Georgia had a smaller population. New Hampshire's government was so poor that it could not afford to send delegates to the Constitutional Convention. Only when John Langdon offered to pay for his and Nicholas Gilman's expenses were the two men able to go. Langdon and Gilman didn't reach Philadelphia until late July, two months after the meeting opened.

Although many of its citizens feared that the new federal government would be too powerful, by a very close vote New Hampshire ratified the Constitution on June 21, 1788. This vote placed the Constitution into effect and made New Hampshire our ninth state. Since 1808 Concord has been the capital of New Hampshire, which because of its vast deposits of the rock is nicknamed the Granite State.

NEW HAMPSHIRE

Name	Birth Date	Age at Signing	Marriage(s)	Children	Death Date	Age at Death
John Langdon	June 26, 1741	46	Elizabeth Sherburne	2	September 18, 1819	78
Nicholas Gilman	August 3, 1755	32	Didn't marry	0	May 2, 1814	58

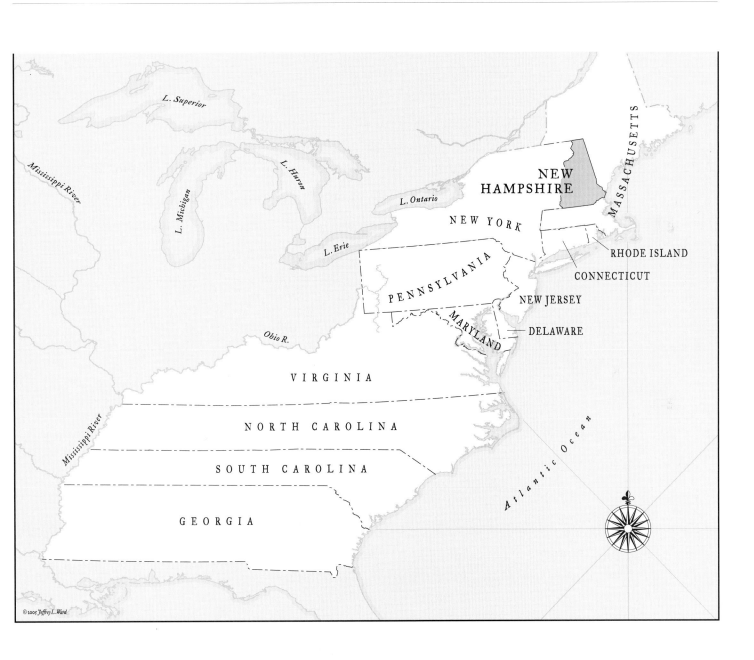

© 2005 Jeffrey L. Ward

JOHN LANGDON
"The National Government Is Mine"

John Langdon

JOHN LANGDON WAS BORN on a farm near Portsmouth, New Hampshire, on June 26, 1741. He attended school in Portsmouth, then found work in a countinghouse and also shipped off on several trading voyages. The money he made helped him become a successful merchant and shipbuilder. By his early thirties, Langdon was said to be the New Hampshire Colony's richest merchant.

Wealthy merchants generally sided with the British in Revolutionary days, but Langdon's heart was with his countrymen. On December 14, 1774, he and fellow New Hampshire patriot John Sullivan led four hundred men in an assault on a British fort at the entrance of Portsmouth Harbor. In one of the first warlike acts against the British before the actual outbreak of hostilities, the Americans took the fort's British guards prisoner and seized cannons and gunpowder.

Langdon's political career began in the mid-1770s, when he served in both the New Hampshire legislature and in the Continental Congress. He temporarily gave up his political career to become a soldier, taking part in campaigns in New York and Rhode Island. In addition, Langdon built ships for the new American navy, including the *Ranger*, which naval hero John Paul Jones commanded. In the summer of 1777, the *Ranger* became the first warship to fly the new American flag, the "Stars and Stripes."

In 1777 thirty-six-year-old John Langdon married sixteen-year-old Elizabeth Sherburne, cousin to Henry Sherburne, whose leg was shattered in the cannonball incident involving Rufus King. One of John and Elizabeth's children died young, but the other, a daughter, reached adulthood.

Following the war, John Langdon returned to politics. In 1785 he was elected governor of New Hampshire, a position he would hold several times over the next twenty-seven years. Then in 1787 the legislature sent Langdon and Nicholas Gilman to the Constitutional Convention, with Langdon personally paying their expenses because the state couldn't afford to do so. Langdon spoke more than twenty times during the debates. Disturbed by delegates who claimed that the Constitution would take too much power from the states, he explained to them, "The general and state governments are not enemies to each other, but different institutions for the good of the people of America. As one of the people, I can say, the national government is mine, the state government is mine."

John Langdon signed the Constitution and was instrumental in winning New Hampshire's approval in June 1788. A few months later, he was elected as one of the first members of the new U.S. Senate. His fellow senators chose Langdon to count the electoral votes and then inform George Washington that he had been elected first president of the United States under the Constitution, which Langdon did by sending Washington a note.

Langdon represented New Hampshire in the U.S. Senate for twelve years until 1801. He returned home to sit in the state legislature from 1801 to 1805. Langdon then served as the Granite State's governor from 1805 to 1809, and again from 1810 to 1812. For many years, New Hampshire's capital had moved from place to place. Governor Langdon convinced the New Hampshire legislature to make Concord the permanent state capital.

John Langdon remained in politics until he was seventy-one. In 1812 he finally stepped down as governor and also refused a nomination to run for vice president of the United States. He spent his last few years at his mansion in Portsmouth, where he died at age seventy-eight on September 18, 1819.

NICHOLAS GILMAN
"It Was Done by Bargain and Compromise"

Nicholas Gilman

ONE OF EIGHT CHILDREN, Nicholas Gilman was born in Exeter, New Hampshire, on August 3, 1755. In his youth, he attended schools in Exeter and worked in his father's general store.

After the Revolution began, Nicholas volunteered for the Continental Army. He served throughout the conflict and for a while was on George Washington's staff. At the Battle of Yorktown, which ended major fighting, General Washington sent Gilman to find out the number of troops the British were surrendering.

In 1783 Nicholas's father died, leaving him property. Nicholas invested in a store in Baltimore, Maryland, but it soon failed. Realizing that the life of a merchant was not for him, Nicholas decided to enter politics.

Americans today often complain that many politicians win office only because of their money and good looks. Things were no different in the country's early days. With his blond hair and blue eyes, Gilman had the reputation of being the most handsome man in New Hampshire. His influential family and good looks helped him win appointment to the Continental Congress. He served from 1786 to 1788, but his attendance was poor, and many of his colleagues felt that he had an inflated idea of his own importance. In fact, they sarcastically nicknamed him Congress Gilman, because he acted as if he owned Congress.

In 1787 Gilman was chosen to attend the Constitutional Convention. Although he made no speeches at the proceedings, he became convinced that the Constitution was the only thing that could save the nation. On September 18, 1787, the day after he signed the document, Gilman wrote to a friend:

> [The Constitution] is the best that could meet the unanimous concurrence of the states in convention. It was done by bargain and compromise, yet, notwithstanding its imperfections, on the adoption of it depends, in my feeble judgment, whether we shall become

a respectable nation or a people torn to pieces by commotions and rendered contemptible for ages.

Gilman then performed his greatest service to his country by working for New Hampshire to ratify the Constitution, which it did in June 1788 by a 57–47 vote. For the nation, this meant that the Constitution had gone into effect. For Gilman, his involvement with the Constitution was a turning point in his career.

Nicholas Gilman spent the second half of his life living up to his nickname by serving in Congress for many years. In 1789 he was elected to the U.S. House of Representatives, where he held a seat until 1797. Following a stint in his state leg-

islature, he was elected to represent New Hampshire in the U.S. Senate, taking office in 1805.

That year he had a serious political quarrel with his older brother John Taylor Gilman, who had governed New Hampshire for many years. The brothers belonged to different political parties, and in the 1805 election for governor Nicholas supported John Langdon, his friend and fellow signer of the Constitution. Nicholas helped Langdon sweep his brother out of office as the state's chief executive.

Nicholas Gilman served in the Senate for the last nine years of his life. On his way back to New Hampshire from Washington, D.C., following a Senate session, he suffered a sudden illness. He died in Philadelphia, the city where he had signed the Constitution, on May 2, 1814. Gilman, who had never married, was fifty-eight years old at the time of his death.

X. VIRGINIA

In the spring of 1607 three small ships, carrying approximately one hundred Englishmen, arrived about midway along what is now the East Coast of the United States. The Englishmen founded Jamestown, America's first permanent English town. The colony where Jamestown was located was called Virginia, in honor of England's Queen Elizabeth I, the "Virgin Queen."

The first of England's thirteen American colonies, Virginia was the scene of many noteworthy events in early America. According to a famous story, the life of Jamestown leader Captain John Smith was saved by the Native American girl Pocahontas. The House of Burgesses, the first legislature in the thirteen colonies composed of elected representatives, met at Jamestown in 1619. Thomas Jefferson wrote the Declaration of Independence while his fellow Virginian George Washington led American troops to victory in the Revolutionary War.

By 1787 Virginia was by far the most populous state. Of its 650,000 people, about 280,000 were slaves who grew tobacco and did other work on Virginia farms and plantations. Virginians played leading roles at the Constitutional Convention. George Washington served as convention president. James Madison designed the Virginia, or Large-State, Plan.

On June 25, 1788, Virginia became the tenth state to join the Union by approving the Constitution. Virginia is sometimes called the Mother of Presidents because eight U.S. presidents—George Washington, Thomas Jefferson, James Madison, James Monroe, William Henry Harrison, John Tyler, Zachary Taylor, and Woodrow Wilson—were born there. Richmond has been Virginia's capital since 1780.

VIRGINIA

Name	Birth Date	Age at Signing	Marriage(s)	Children	Death Date	Age at Death
James Madison	March 16, 1751	36	Dolley Payne Todd	0	June 28, 1836	85
George Washington	February 22, 1732	55	Martha Custis	0	December 14, 1799	67
John Blair	1732	About 55	Jean Balfour	2	August 31, 1800	About 68

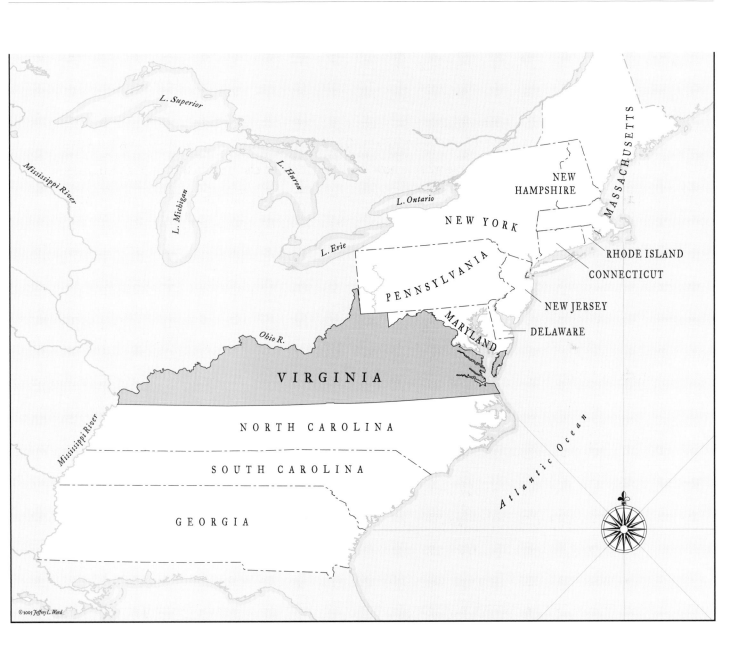

© 2005 Jeffrey L. Ward

JAMES MADISON
The "Father of the Constitution"

James Madison Jr.

THE OLDEST OF TWELVE CHILDREN, James Madison was born on March 16, 1751, at the home of his mother's parents in Port Conway, Virginia. He grew up at Montpelier, his family's plantation in Virginia's Orange County, which remained his lifelong residence.

James, who tended to be a sickly and frail youth, was sent to a boarding school at the age of eleven. After five years there and two years studying at home with a tutor, eighteen-year-old James Madison journeyed three hundred miles northward to attend what is now Princeton University in New Jersey. An outstanding student, he graduated in 1771 after just two years of study.

Madison considered becoming a minister, but his voice was too soft for him to preach. He tried to study law but disliked it. What interested him most was politics. During the 1770s he served in Virginia's Revolutionary government, helping to write its first state constitution and becoming friends with Thomas Jefferson.

At the age of twenty-eight, Madison was elected to represent Virginia in the Continental Congress. While serving there from 1780 to 1783, he helped organize the U.S. government under the Articles of Confederation. Back home in Virginia, Madison served in the state legislature from 1784 to 1786.

In 1786 Virginia sent Madison to the Annapolis Convention. There he worked to bring about the Constitutional Convention, at which he also represented his state. Madison impressed his fellow delegates in Philadelphia with his enormous knowledge of government. On May 29, the Virginia delegation presented the Virginia Plan, which was mostly Madison's creation. Many of its proposals were incorporated into the Constitution, and even those that weren't provided a starting point for debate.

Despite being a poor speaker, Madison addressed the convention more than

150 times as he argued for a strong federal government. Only Gouverneur Morris and James Wilson spoke more often. Madison also kept notes that provide the best record we have of the proceedings. For all his contributions, Madison is remembered as the "Father of the Constitution."

To help the Constitution gain acceptance, Madison and two New Yorkers, Alexander Hamilton and John Jay, wrote a series of essays in its defense. These eighty-five Federalist Papers, of which fifty-one were written by Hamilton, twenty-nine by Madison, and five by Jay, were published in newspapers beginning in 1787 and also appeared as a book called *The Federalist*. The essays helped win approval for the Constitution throughout America and are still considered the clearest explanation of the document's principles.

James Madison played a major role in convincing leaders in his home state to approve the Constitution by a close vote on June 25, 1788. A big objection of the Constitution's foes was that it had no bill of rights to protect such basic rights as freedom of speech and freedom of religion. Madison did something about this, too. In the U.S. House of Representatives, where he served from 1789 to 1797, he drafted and fought for approval of what became the first ten amendments to the Constitution, also known as the Bill of Rights.

James Madison remained a bachelor until middle age. In May 1794 the forty-three-year-old Congressman was introduced to Dolley Payne Todd, a twenty-six-year-old widow who had been born in North Carolina but grew up in Virginia. The two were married on September 15, 1794. James and Dolley Madison had no children together, but a son from her first marriage, Payne Todd, became James's stepson.

In 1801 Thomas Jefferson became the third president and appointed his friend James Madison secretary of state. Jefferson's wife had died, so Dolley Madison often served as hostess at the president's White House events. James Madison then followed Jefferson in the nation's highest office, serving as our fourth president from 1809 to 1817.

During Madison's presidency, the United States and Britain fought a second war, called the War of 1812, from that year until 1815. In August 1814 the British invaded Washington, D.C., burning the U.S. Capitol, the White House, and other government buildings. President Madison was away during the skirmishing. Dolley Madison gathered up and rescued numerous documents as well as a portrait of George Washington before fleeing the White House at the last moment.

After Madison left office, he and Dolley retired to Montpelier. For the last ten years of his life, Madison, who once said that "a well-instructed people alone can be a permanently free people," served as rector, or president, of the University of Virginia. The Father of the Constitution was the last surviving signer of the great document when he died at Montpelier on June 28, 1836, at the age of eighty-five.

GEORGE WASHINGTON
"The Best Constitution That Can Be Obtained"

GEORGE WASHINGTON WAS BORN in Virginia's Westmoreland County on February 22, 1732, the oldest of six children of Augustine (called Gus) and Mary Ball Washington. While moving about eastern Virginia with his family, George attended school for a total of about seven years. The tall, athletic youth loved to hunt in the woods and ride his horse when he was not in school or working at his farm chores.

George's youngest sister died as a baby, and his father died when George was only eleven. George helped his widowed mother care for his remaining sister and three brothers. By 1746 George wanted to join the English navy, but his mother refused to grant her fourteen-year-old son permission because of the hardships of a sailor's life. Since he had a talent for mathematics and mapmaking, George then decided to become a surveyor. Sixteen-year-old Washington helped survey the Virginia wilderness for a wealthy landowner, and the next year he helped lay out the streets of the new town of Alexandria, Virginia. The youth spent his wages on land, and by the age of eighteen he owned about 1,500 acres and was on the road to wealth.

Washington began his military career during the French and Indian War (1754–63). Like many other colonists, he fought for Britain in its struggle with France for control of North America. In fact, the war's first battle occurred on May 28, 1754, when Lieutenant Colonel Washington and his troops defeated French forces at the Battle of Great Meadows near what is now Uniontown, Pennsylvania. Washington became known for his bravery during the war. "I luckily escaped without a wound, though I had four bullets through my coat and two horses shot under me," he wrote about one battle.

Washington's participation in the war, won eventually by England, ended in late 1758. On January 6 of the new year he married a widow named Martha Custis.

The couple settled at Mount Vernon, George Washington's home in Virginia's Fairfax County. Although George and Martha Washington had no children together, he adopted her children from her earlier marriage, a boy named Jackie and a girl named Patsy.

For the next fifteen years, George Washington farmed, conducted business deals, and attended balls and fox hunts like other wealthy Virginia planters. He also served in the Virginia lawmaking body, the House of Burgesses.

After the troubles with the mother country began, Washington was sent to represent Virginia at the Continental Congress in Philadelphia. There, on June 15, 1775, he was elected commander in chief of the newly formed Continental Army. Rarely has a commander overcome such great odds. Washington's largest army during the war contained 20,000 men, compared to 50,000 for the British. To make things worse, Congress could not afford to arm, feed, or clothe its troops

properly. At times, American soldiers went barefoot and raided beehives and shot squirrels to keep from starving.

Realizing that his army wasn't yet strong enough to win a big battle, General Washington mostly fought small battles for several years while training his men. Finally, he had a chance to fight the giant battle for which he had prepared for six years. With French help, his forces pounded the British at Yorktown, Virginia, in October 1781. This victory won America's independence, and secured Washington's reputation as America's greatest hero of the Revolution.

Following the signing of the peace treaty in 1783, Washington resigned his command and returned to Mount Vernon. He thought his public life had ended, but a new phase of it was just beginning. Washington was among the American leaders who knew that the country needed a stronger central government. In 1785 he hosted the Mount Vernon Conference, which led to the Annapolis Convention the next year and the Constitutional Convention in 1787.

As their first order of business the delegates to the Philadephia gathering elected Washington convention president. He said little during the convention, yet his presence lent importance to the meeting and helped minimize disputes. Washington did make one recommendation. On the last day of the convention, he spoke in favor of Nathaniel Gorham's proposal that the House of Representatives have one member for each 30,000 inhabitants. With Washington's backing, the proposal was passed unanimously.

Washington was pleased with the new governmental framework, calling it "the best Constitution that can be obtained." His signature on the document was an important factor in its eventually being approved by all thirteen states. As everyone had expected, Washington was elected to become the nation's first president under the Constitution. While holding office from 1789 to 1797, he helped prevent the states from fighting one another and also kept the nation out of war.

George Washington lived less than three years after retiring from the presidency. The "Father of Our Country" died of a throat infection at Mount Vernon on December 14, 1799, at the age of sixty-seven. In later life Washington had turned against slavery. According to the terms of his will, his slaves were freed following the death of his wife Martha in 1802.

JOHN BLAIR
A Respected Supreme Court Justice

John Blair —

JOHN BLAIR WAS BORN sometime in 1732 in Williamsburg, which served as Virginia's capital from 1699 to 1780. His father was a prominent lawmaker who twice served as the Virginia Colony's acting governor. An uncle of John's had founded and served as the first president of the College of William and Mary in Williamsburg. Begun in 1693, the College of William and Mary today is the country's second-oldest college. Only Harvard, which dates from 1636, is older.

The red-haired youth attended his hometown college. He graduated with honors from the College of William and Mary in 1754, then studied law in England for about two years. While in the mother country, he married Jean Balfour on the day after Christmas of 1756. The couple, who would have two daughters, remained in England for a while and then sailed to America.

Back in Williamsburg, John Blair practiced law and entered politics. He served in Virginia's House of Burgesses during Revolutionary times, becoming friends with George Washington, Patrick Henry, and other Virginians who opposed British injustice. Blair was a member of the committee that drew up Virginia's first state constitution in 1776, and two years later, he began a long career as a judge.

His reputation as an honest and fair judge helped win Blair a place on the Virginia delegation to the Constitutional Convention. It was reported that he attended the meetings faithfully but made no speeches and didn't serve on any committees. However, his support for the Constitution was crucial. Without Blair, Virginia, which was the most populous of the thirteen states, would have had only two signers.

After signing the Constitution, Blair returned to Virginia with George Washington. On the way home, the two men narrowly avoided disaster when a bridge began to collapse beneath them. Fortunately the two Virginians escaped unhurt on foot, but their carriage barely avoided a steep plunge into the waters below. George Washington wrote in his diary: "I [was] in company with Mr. Blair who I invited to a seat in my Carriage. Carriage had a very narrow escape. One of my horses fell 15 feet at least, the other very near following which had it happened would have taken the Carriage along with him."

In September of 1789, just a few months after taking office as our first president, George Washington nominated Blair for a seat on the new U.S. Supreme Court. Two days later the Senate confirmed Blair's appointment. While serving on the nation's highest court for more than six years, Blair helped establish the independence and importance of our federal court system.

John Blair retired from the Supreme Court due to illness in early 1796. He spent his last years in poor health at his home in Williamsburg, where he died on August 31, 1800, at the age of about sixty-eight.

XI. NEW YORK

The region's first colonists were the Dutch, who founded Fort Orange in 1624 and New Amsterdam the next year. The Dutch introduced the *Sinterklaas* tradition to America and such foods as *koolsla* and *olykoecks*.

The English seized the region in 1664, naming it New York for the English Duke of York and Albany (later King James II). They also changed the names of Fort Orange to Albany and New Amsterdam to New York City. English children said the Dutch name *Sinterklaas* so quickly that his name became "Santa Claus." The Dutch food *koolsla* became known as coleslaw, and *olykoecks* as "doughnuts."

During the Revolutionary War about a hundred battles took place in New York. Schoolteacher Nathan Hale, working as a spy for General Washington, was captured by the British near New York City. He reportedly said, "I only regret that I have but one life to lose for my country," before he was hanged.

With three hundred thousand people, New York was tied with Maryland for fifth place in population in 1787. Two of New York's delegates to the Constitutional Convention—John Lansing and Robert Yates—left early because they thought the new government would be too powerful. That left Alexander Hamilton as the state's lone signer.

New York became the eleventh state by narrowly approving the Constitution on July 26, 1788. Albany has been the state capital since 1797. New York is nicknamed the Empire State because George Washington once predicted that it would become the center of an American empire. He was right. Today the Empire State ranks behind only California and Texas in population, and it is a leader in manufacturing, finance, publishing, and radio and TV broadcasting.

NEW YORK

Name	Birth Date	Age at Signing	Marriage(s)	Children	Death Date	Age at Death
ALEXANDER HAMILTON	January 11, 1755	32	Betsy Schuyler	8	July 12, 1804	49

© 2005 Jeffrey L. Ward

ALEXANDER HAMILTON
"To Render the Constitution of the Federal Government Adequate"

Alexander Hamilton

ALEXANDER HAMILTON WAS BORN on Nevis, a British-ruled island in the West Indies. His birth date was January 11, 1755, but it is sometimes wrongly listed as 1757 because he later shaved two years off his age to make himself seem younger than he actually was.

When Alexander was ten, his father abandoned the family. Several days after Alexander's thirteenth birthday, his mother died. About that time, Alexander was apprenticed to Nicholas Cruger, a merchant on St. Croix, one of the Virgin Islands in the West Indies. In 1771, Cruger had to go to New York. He had such a high opinion of sixteen-year-old Alexander's ability that he left him in charge of his firm's St. Croix office. Upon his return a few months later, Cruger spoke of making young Hamilton a business partner, but Alexander dreamed of attending college in America.

In the summer of 1772, a hurricane slammed into St. Croix. Seventeen-year-old Alexander Hamilton wrote a letter to a newspaper providing a marvelous description of the giant storm:

> Good God! What horror and destruction. It seemed as if a total dissolution of nature was taking place. The roaring of the sea and wind, the glare of almost perpetual lightning, the crash of the falling houses, and the ear-piercing shrieks of the distressed were sufficient to strike astonishment into angels.

Realizing that Alexander deserved a good education, his friends and relatives raised money and sent him to America in October 1772. For a while he attended school in Elizabeth, New Jersey, where he was often invited into the home of William Livingston, a much older man who would one day sign the Constitution with him.

Hamilton enrolled at New York City's King's College (now Columbia University) in the fall of 1773, a period when America was moving toward war with Great Britain. He began to write articles and make speeches siding with the patriots and opposing British injustice. People were astonished at the young man's brilliance, and his fame as a speaker and writer spread.

After the Revolution began, Hamilton joined the Continental Army. He fought heroically in New York, New Jersey, and Virginia, and for much of the war served as George Washington's most important aide. The general depended on Hamilton to help him write letters and assist him in organizing the army.

In late 1780 Hamilton married Elizabeth Schuyler of New York. Betsy and Alexander had eight children. At the end of the war Hamilton became an attorney, opening a Wall Street law office in New York City. During the 1780s he also served in the Continental Congress and the New York state legislature.

Hamilton represented New York at the Annapolis Convention in 1786. There he pushed through a recommendation that a meeting be held in Philadelphia the next May "to render the Constitution of the Federal Government adequate to the [needs] of the Union."

Despite his brilliance, Hamilton had little influence at the Philadelphia convention. For one thing, New York's other delegates, John Lansing and Robert Yates, opposed a strong federal government and could swing their state's vote against Hamilton. Also, Hamilton had some unpopular ideas, arguing that the president, senators, and Supreme Court justices should hold office for life. Because Lansing and Yates left the convention early, Hamilton was the only New Yorker to sign the Constitution.

The "Little Lion," as Hamilton was called, waged a relentless campaign for the approval of the Constitution. He wrote the bulk (fifty-one) of the newspaper essays called the Federalist Papers, which urged ratification of the Constitution, with James Madison and John Jay producing the remaining thirty-four. And his efforts at the ratification convention in Poughkeepsie, New York, were instrumental in his state narrowly approving the Constitution on July 26, 1788.

Following his election as the nation's first president, George Washington chose his former aide to be the first secretary of the treasury. During more than five years in that post, Hamilton strengthened the nation's finances and helped organize its banking system. In 1796 he wrote much of the famous Farewell Address for the retiring President Washington.

Hamilton practiced law in New York City in his later years. An outspoken man of strong opinions, the Little Lion made several political enemies. One of them was Aaron Burr, whom Hamilton helped prevent from becoming president in 1800 and governor of New York four years later. Burr's hatred of Hamilton became so intense that he challenged him to a pistol duel.

Early on the morning of July 11, 1804, the two men met at Weehawken, New Jersey. In their duel Burr shot Hamilton, who died the next day at the age of forty-nine. To this day, Alexander Hamilton and Benjamin Franklin are the most famous of the signers of the Constitution who never became president. A portrait of Alexander Hamilton, Founding Father and first secretary of the treasury, can be seen on U.S. ten-dollar bills.

XII. NORTH CAROLINA

England's first North American settlement was established along North Carolina's coast in 1585, but the colony was soon abandoned. More English colonists, including a couple named Eleanor and Ananias Dare, arrived in mid-1587. On August 18, Eleanor gave birth to Virginia Dare, the first English child born in America. The colonists soon vanished, however. Perhaps they went to live with the Indians, but exactly what became of the "Lost Colony" is not known. With the founding of Jamestown in 1607, Virginia and not North Carolina became England's first permanent American colony.

The first permanent colonists in what became North Carolina moved there from Virginia in the 1650s. At the time the region was part of what was called Carolana ("Land of Charles" in Latin), to honor King Charles I. Later the spelling was changed slightly, and the territory split into North and South Carolina.

In colonial times and for many years after, North Carolinians led the world in producing "naval stores." These were tar, turpentine, and other products from pine trees used in building and repairing ships. Many other North Carolinians were farmers who grew corn, beans, rice, and a little tobacco. By 1787 North Carolina ranked behind only Virginia and Pennsylvania in its population of 360,000, of whom approximately 100,000 were slaves.

So many North Carolinians opposed the Constitution that a convention of its leaders rejected the document in the summer of 1788. Not until November 21, 1789, did North Carolina become our twelfth state. Since 1792 Raleigh has been the capital of North Carolina, which is nicknamed the Tar Heel State. According to one story, North Carolina tar workers had such difficulty washing the sticky substance off their hands and feet that people jokingly referred to them as "Tar Heels."

NORTH CAROLINA

Name	Birth Date	Age at Signing	Marriage(s)	Children	Death Date	Age at Death
HUGH WILLIAMSON	December 5, 1735	51	Maria Apthorpe	2	May 22, 1819	83
RICHARD DOBBS SPAIGHT	March 25, 1758	29	Mary Leach	3	September 6, 1802	44
WILLIAM BLOUNT	March 26, 1749	38	Mary Grainger	8	March 21, 1800	50

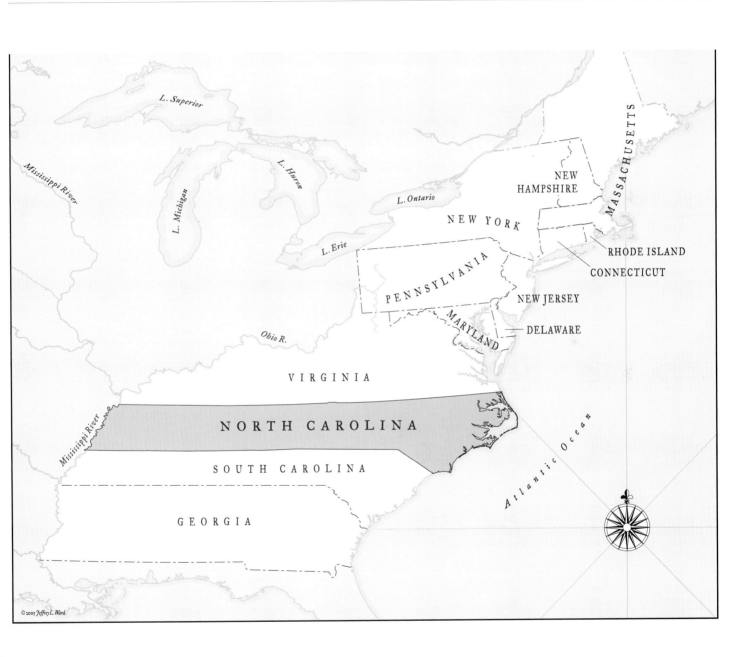

© 2005 Jeffrey L. Ward

HUGH WILLIAMSON
"More Free and More Perfect than Any Form of Government"

Hu Williamson

IN 1717 A YOUNG CHILD named Mary Davison was sailing from Ireland to America with her father. Their ship was captured by Edward Teach, known as Blackbeard, but fortunately the famous pirate with the long braided beard let the Davisons go. Mary grew up, married a man from Ireland named John Williamson, and had ten children. Hugh, the oldest son, was born not far from Philadelphia in Chester County, Pennsylvania, on December 5, 1735.

A brilliant child, Hugh studied Greek and Latin at an academy. Later he attended what is now the University of Pennsylvania, receiving his diploma at the college's first graduation in 1757.

Williamson then began his career—or rather, careers. He became a minister and preached for about two years until he realized that the pulpit was not for him. From 1760 to 1763 he worked as a mathematics professor at his old college. Next he decided to become a doctor. For about four years he studied medicine in Europe, receiving his medical degree in 1768 from the University of Utrecht in the Netherlands. Returning to America, he set up practice in Philadelphia.

Meanwhile, Williamson had also turned his attention to other sciences. He became friends with Ben Franklin and performed electrical experiments with him. In addition, he became interested in climate and astronomy. Over his long life he wrote many papers and books on subjects ranging from comets to electric eels. Among his theories, Williamson believed that the universe contained, as he wrote, "five million worlds all inhabited by rational beings."

In 1773 Dr. Williamson was asked to visit England to raise money for the school that became the University of Delaware. Late that year he was in Boston waiting for his ship to sail when he witnessed the Boston Tea Party. Called before officials in England, he explained that British actions were sparking a rebellion in

America. After the war began, Williamson was returning home when the British captured his ship, but he and a fellow passenger managed to escape to shore in a rowboat.

Philadelphia fell into British hands in September 1777, so around that time Hugh Williamson moved to Edenton, North Carolina, where he resumed his medical career. During the war he served as a physician to North Carolina troops. As the war ended, Williamson added politics to his list of interests. In 1782 he was elected to the North Carolina legislature. During the next few years he served in the legislature and also represented North Carolina in the Continental Congress.

In 1787 Williamson was elected to represent North Carolina at the Constitutional Convention, where he sat on five different committees and made many

suggestions. For example, various delegates wanted the term of office for senators to be four, seven, or nine years, or even a lifetime appointment. Williamson was the first to propose a six-year term, which was the final choice. He later campaigned for ratification in North Carolina, calling the new Constitution "more free and more perfect than any form of government that has ever been adopted by any nation."

The fifty-three-year-old physician, lawmaker, and scientist married a New York woman, Maria Apthorpe, in January 1789. Hugh and Maria had two sons. From the year of his marriage to 1793, Williamson represented the Tar Heel State in the country's new House of Representatives. In 1793 he gave up politics and moved with his family to New York City.

Sadly, Maria died shortly after the birth of their second son, and both of Williamson's sons died as young men. Hugh Williamson spent his last years writing and donating his time and money to such good causes as an orphanage and a hospital. He was driving his carriage with his niece in New York City when he suffered a heart attack or stroke and died on May 22, 1819, at the age of eighty-three.

RICHARD DOBBS SPAIGHT
He Didn't Miss a Session

Rich? Dobbs Spaight.

RICHARD DOBBS SPAIGHT WAS BORN in New Bern, North Carolina, on March 25, 1758. He came from a prominent family. His father served as treasurer and secretary to North Carolina's royal governor. Richard's uncle, Arthur Dobbs, *was* the governor of the North Carolina Colony.

Three days after Richard's seventh birthday, his uncle the governor died. At the age of eight, Richard lost both of his parents. His guardians sent the young orphan abroad. Richard received an outstanding education, first in Ireland and later at the University of Glasgow in Scotland.

Young Spaight returned to North Carolina in 1778, during the Revolutionary War. Despite having spent the last decade in the British Isles, he sided with his native land. In 1779, at the age of only twenty-one, he was elected to the North Carolina legislature. He then decided to fight for his country. He joined the North Carolina militia as an aide to General Richard Caswell and served at the Battle of Camden in South Carolina in 1780. He returned to politics at the war's end. For much of the 1780s Spaight sat either in the state legislature or in the Continental Congress.

In 1787 Spaight was chosen to represent North Carolina at the Constitutional Convention. He was one of only a few delegates who didn't miss a single session. Soon after the meeting opened on May 25, Spaight proposed that, even after they approved a matter, the delegates should be allowed to change their minds until the last moment. His suggestion was approved, but other proposals he put forward weren't. For example, he wanted the terms of the president as well as U.S. senators to be seven years.

Spaight signed the document on September 17, then went home to help secure ratification. That proved to be a difficult struggle, for of the original states, only Rhode Island took longer than North Carolina to approve the Constitution.

In 1792 Spaight was elected governor of the Tar Heel State. He held his state's highest office from that year until 1795. During the last year of his governorship he opened the University of North Carolina at Chapel Hill. Also in 1795 he married a Pennsylvania woman, Mary Leach, with whom he had three children.

From 1798 to 1801 Spaight represented North Carolina in the U.S. House of Representatives. He then served as a state senator, which turned out to be his last public office. Spaight and rival North Carolina lawmaker John Stanly engaged in a bitter feud, with Stanly accusing Spaight of having faked illness to avoid voting on controversial issues while in Congress. Spaight, whose health had been failing for several years, was incensed, especially because he took pride in his attendance record as a lawmaker. The argument became so heated that one of the men (it is not clear who) challenged the other to a pistol duel.

Stanly and Spaight met behind a building on the outskirts of New Bern on September 5, 1802. Reportedly Spaight was so ill by this time that he could hardly grip his pistol. As would happen to Alexander Hamilton less than two years later, Spaight was critically wounded. He died the following day at the age of only forty-four. Richard Dobbs Spaight left behind his widow Mary and their three children, including six-year-old Richard Dobbs Spaight Jr., who grew up to govern the Tar Heel State in 1835–36.

WILLIAM BLOUNT

He Was a Rascal

THE FOUNDING FATHERS ARE OFTEN portrayed as heroes who far exceed our current politicians in brilliance and honesty. That may have been true of some of them, but anyone who is tempted to place all the founders on a pedestal should examine the career of William Blount.

The oldest of eight children, William was born on March 26, 1749, at Rosefield, a family estate in North Carolina's Bertie County. He grew up at Blount Hall, a cotton and tobacco plantation near New Bern, North Carolina. William's father was a rich landowner, merchant, and politician in New Bern, which was one of the towns that served as North Carolina's colonial capital.

Although there was no school at New Bern, William received an outstanding education. He was taught by his parents and by tutors. Shortly after William's fourteenth birthday, his mother died. As the oldest son, William began to accompany his father as he traveled through North Carolina, buying and selling land. William grew up to value land as the most precious possession a person could have.

In 1776, his father arranged for William to be appointed paymaster for a battalion of North Carolina soldiers in the Continental Army. William used the position to make large profits selling goods to the soldiers. Somehow he also lost $300,000 of the soldiers' payroll—or so he claimed. In 1778 William married a wealthy young woman named Mary Grainger, who was known as Molsey. The couple settled on a North Carolina estate called Piney Grove and had eight children.

During the 1780s William Blount served in the North Carolina legislature and on and off in the Continental Congress. Over the years he used his position as a lawmaker to make it easier for himself and his relatives to obtain land in North Carolina, Tennessee, and Alabama. Among his illegal and questionable activities, he used false names in land transactions, took possession of real estate he wasn't entitled to, and wheedled the Indians out of their lands. But the good-looking and charming Blount managed to avoid trouble for a long time, and he also became popular with many western settlers who hungered for the Native Americans' land.

In 1787, thirty-eight-year-old William Blount was named to attend the Constitutional Convention. He was pessimistic about the future of the country, which he thought wouldn't last much longer. Blount did not take part in the debates and broke the secrecy rule by sending letters describing the proceedings home to North Carolina. He thought so little of the completed Constitution that at first he refused to sign it.

Gouverneur Morris of Pennsylvania went to work on Blount. Affixing his name to the document didn't mean that Blount approved of it, Morris argued. It

merely meant that he was part of the North Carolina delegation that had helped create the paper. Actually, George Mason and Edmund Randolph of Virginia and Elbridge Gerry of Massachusetts refused to sign the Constitution because they weren't satisfied with it, but Gouverneur Morris was a smooth talker, and Blount reluctantly signed.

Back home, thousands of North Carolinians opposed the Constitution. In the summer of 1788, North Carolina leaders voted not to adopt the Constitution by a large margin. The country wondered: Would North Carolina ever become a state under the new constitution?

William Blount, meanwhile, was becoming convinced that the Constitution was best for the development of the American frontier. He performed what may have been his greatest service for his country when he helped persuade North Carolina leaders to finally adopt the Constitution on November 21, 1789. That day North Carolina became our twelfth state.

In 1790 President Washington appointed Blount governor of the Tennessee Territory, a region North Carolina had recently turned over to the U.S. government. Blount brought his family to Tennessee and served as its territorial governor until 1796, the year Tennessee became our sixteenth state. Blount was then elected as one of Tennessee's first two U.S. senators.

Blount's dishonest land dealings were catching up with him, however. He accumulated colossal land holdings—somewhere around two *million* acres, or about 3,000 square miles. The value of land along the American frontier plunged in the 1790s. Hoping to restore land values, Blount became involved in a complex plot to turn over what are now U.S. lands to the British. Plotting to hand over to another country land that America wanted or owned was a serious crime. Blount's scheme was uncovered, and he was expelled from the Senate. The Founding Father who had destroyed his reputation with his political intrigues and land schemes died in Knoxville, Tennessee, on March 21, 1800, five days before what would have been his fifty-first birthday.

XIII. RHODE ISLAND

Giovanni da Verrazano, an Italian sailing for France, reached what became Rhode Island in 1524, and the Dutch explorer Adriaen Block arrived in 1614. An island in the region resembled the island of Rhodes near Greece, wrote Verrazano, which may be how Rhode Island received its name. Or perhaps the name originated after Block called an island with red clay along its shore Roodt Eylandt, meaning "Red Island" in Dutch.

In 1636 Massachusetts minister Roger Williams was ordered to be shipped back to England for claiming that all people should be allowed to worship as they pleased. Instead he and a few friends escaped to Rhode Island, where Williams founded the colony's first non-Indian town, Providence, in 1636. Under Roger Williams's direction, Providence was the first town in the thirteen colonies to offer complete freedom of worship. Among those who moved to Rhode Island seeking religious freedom was Anne Hutchinson, who in 1638 helped begin Portsmouth. Other colonists called Rhode Island "Rogue Island" because it opened its doors to everyone, but today it is known as the birthplace of religious tolerance in America.

Colonial Rhode Islanders farmed, built ships, hunted whales, and worked as sea captains and merchants. By 1787 the smallest colony in size contained 65,000 people. Only Delaware had a smaller population. Rhode Islanders feared that a new federal government would swallow their little state. They sent no delegates to the Constitutional Convention and were the last to approve the new governmental framework. Not until May 29, 1790, did Rhode Island ratify the Constitution and join the Union.

Providence has been Rhode Island's capital since 1900. Our tiniest state is nicknamed the Ocean State and also Little Rhody.

RHODE ISLAND

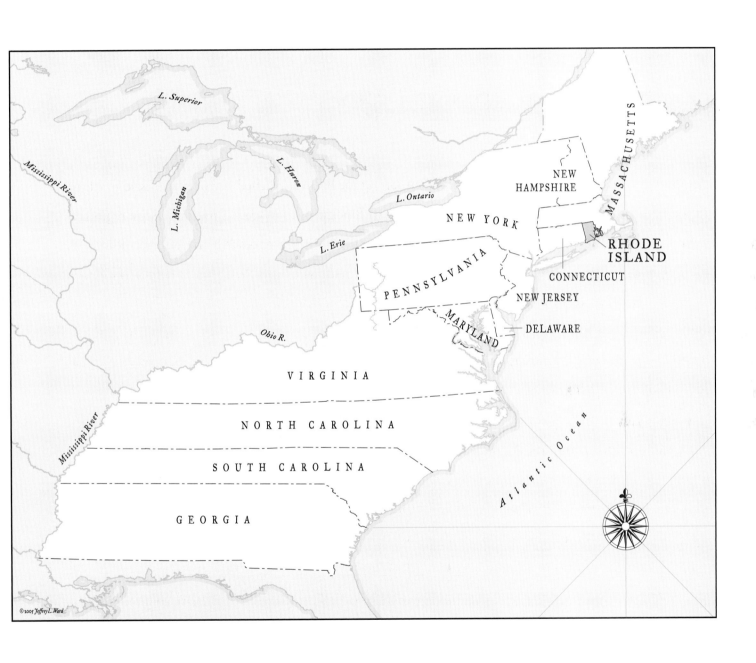

L. Superior

Mississippi River

L. Michigan

L. Huron

L. Ontario

L. Erie

NEW HAMPSHIRE

MASSACHUSETTS

NEW YORK

RHODE ISLAND

PENNSYLVANIA

CONNECTICUT

NEW JERSEY

MARYLAND

DELAWARE

Ohio R.

VIRGINIA

Mississippi River

NORTH CAROLINA

SOUTH CAROLINA

Atlantic Ocean

GEORGIA

© 2005 Jeffrey L. Ward

AFTERWORD

"It Is a Rising Sun!"

As the last delegates signed the Constitution on September 17, 1787, Ben Franklin made one of his most memorable remarks. During the convention, the eighty-one-year-old statesman pointed out, George Washington had sat in a chair that featured a carved image of the sun on it. Often in the course of the four-month-long proceedings, Franklin had wondered whether the chairmaker had intended the sun to be rising or setting. Now Franklin was so filled with hope about the young nation's future that he at last had the answer.

"It is a rising sun!" he proclaimed.

Subsequent events have borne out Ben's optimism. On June 21, 2005, the Constitution celebrated its two hundred and seventeenth anniversary since New Hampshire placed it into effect by becoming the ninth state in the summer of 1788. Franklin would be happy to know that for more than two centuries the nation has endured and flourished, thanks largely to the document he and the other founders created. During those years the Constitution has helped the nation survive perilous times: the Civil War, which cost more American lives than any other war ever fought; the assassination of Presidents Abraham Lincoln, James A. Garfield, William McKinley, and John F. Kennedy; World War I; the Great Depression; World War II; and, more recently, the September 11, 2001, terrorist attacks in which two jetliners destroyed the twin towers of the World Trade Center in New York City and a third plane rammed into the Pentagon outside Washington, D.C.

Like his colleagues, Ben knew that the Constitution wasn't perfect. The founders also realized that they couldn't see into the future and plan for changing times. That was why they built into the Constitution the process by which the document could be amended or changed. In all the years since it took effect, the Constitution has been amended twenty-seven times, including the first ten amendments, which are known as the Bill of Rights. The amendments have helped make the United States a more democratic country, with greater participation in government by its people.

For example, the Thirteenth Amendment, abolishing slavery, took effect at the end of the Civil War in 1865. The Fourteenth and Fifteenth Amendments, ratified not long after, guaranteed the former slaves their rights as citizens and their voting rights, respectively. The Nineteenth Amendment, ratified in 1920, granted women the right to vote, while the Twenty-sixth Amendment, which took effect in 1971, lowered the voting age to eighteen years. In the decades ahead, there will undoubtedly be more amendments to make certain that our Constitution keeps pace with an ever-changing nation.

Among the items visitors to Independence Hall in Philadelphia can see is the actual chair George Washington sat in when he presided over the Constitutional Convention. There, on the top of it, is the sun that Ben Franklin wondered about as he attended the convention meetings so long ago. If you view the carving as a work of art, you can't tell whether the sun is supposed to be rising or setting. But if you think of it as representing the United States, you will probably agree with Ben Franklin:

"It is a rising sun!"

We the People

of the United States, in Order to form a more perfect Union, establish Justice, insure domestic Tranquility, provide for the common defence, promote the general Welfare, and secure the Blessings of Liberty to ourselves and our Posterity, do ordain and establish this Constitution for the United States of America.

Article. I.

Section. 1. All legislative Powers herein granted shall be vested in a Congress of the United States, which shall consist of a Senate and House of Representatives.

Section. 2. The House of Representatives shall be composed of Members chosen every second Year by the People of the several States, and the Electors in each State shall have the Qualifications requisite for Electors of the most numerous Branch of the State Legislature.

No Person shall be a Representative who shall not have attained to the Age of twenty five Years, and been seven Years a Citizen of the United States, and who shall not, when elected, be an Inhabitant of that State in which he shall be chosen.

Representatives and direct Taxes shall be apportioned among the several States which may be included within this Union, according to their respective Numbers, which shall be determined by adding to the whole Number of free Persons, including those bound to Service for a Term of Years, and excluding Indians not taxed, three fifths of all other Persons. The actual Enumeration shall be made within three Years after the first Meeting of the Congress of the United States, and within every subsequent Term of ten Years, in such Manner as they shall by Law direct. The Number of Representatives shall not exceed one for every thirty Thousand, but each State shall have at Least one Representative; and until such enumeration shall be made, the State of New Hampshire shall be entitled to chuse three, Massachusetts eight, Rhode Island and Providence Plantations one, Connecticut five, New York six, New Jersey four, Pennsylvania eight, Delaware one, Maryland six, Virginia ten, North Carolina five, South Carolina five, and Georgia three.

When vacancies happen in the Representation from any State, the Executive Authority thereof shall issue Writs of Election to fill such Vacancies.

The House of Representatives shall chuse their Speaker and other Officers; and shall have the sole Power of Impeachment.

Section. 3. The Senate of the United States shall be composed of two Senators from each State, chosen by the Legislature thereof, for six Years; and each Senator shall have one Vote.

Immediately after they shall be assembled in Consequence of the first Election, they shall be divided as equally as may be into three Classes. The Seats of the Senators of the first Class shall be vacated at the Expiration of the second Year, of the second Class at the Expiration of the fourth Year, and of the third Class at the Expiration of the sixth Year, so that one third may be chosen every second Year; and if Vacancies happen by Resignation, or otherwise, during the Recess of the Legislature of any State, the Executive thereof may make temporary Appointments until the next Meeting of the Legislature, which shall then fill such Vacancies.

No Person shall be a Senator who shall not have attained to the Age of thirty Years, and been nine Years a Citizen of the United States, and who shall not, when elected, be an Inhabitant of that State for which he shall be chosen.

The Vice President of the United States shall be President of the Senate, but shall have no Vote, unless they be equally divided.

The Senate shall chuse their other Officers, and also a President pro tempore, in the Absence of the Vice President, or when he shall exercise the Office of President of the United States.

The Senate shall have the sole Power to try all Impeachments. When sitting for that Purpose, they shall be on Oath or Affirmation. When the President of the United States is tried, the Chief Justice shall preside: And no Person shall be convicted without the Concurrence of two thirds of the Members present.

Judgment in Cases of Impeachment shall not extend further than to removal from Office, and disqualification to hold and enjoy any Office of honor, Trust or Profit under the United States: but the Party convicted shall nevertheless be liable and subject to Indictment, Trial, Judgment and Punishment, according to Law.

Section. 4. The Times, Places and Manner of holding Elections for Senators and Representatives, shall be prescribed in each State by the Legislature thereof; but the Congress may at any time by Law make or alter such Regulations, except as to the Places of chusing Senators.

The Congress shall assemble at least once in every Year, and such Meeting shall be on the first Monday in December, unless they shall by Law appoint a different Day.

Section. 5. Each House shall be the Judge of the Elections, Returns and Qualifications of its own Members, and a Majority of each shall constitute a Quorum to do Business; but a smaller Number may adjourn from day to day, and may be authorized to compel the Attendance of absent Members, in such Manner, and under such Penalties as each House may provide.

Each House may determine the Rules of its Proceedings, punish its Members for disorderly Behaviour, and, with the Concurrence of two thirds, expel a Member.

Each House shall keep a Journal of its Proceedings, and from time to time publish the same, excepting such Parts as may in their Judgment require Secrecy; and the Yeas and Nays of the Members of either House on any question shall, at the Desire of one fifth of those Present, be entered on the Journal.

Neither House, during the Session of Congress, shall, without the Consent of the other, adjourn for more than three days, nor to any other Place than that in which the two Houses shall be sitting.

Section. 6. The Senators and Representatives shall receive a Compensation for their Services, to be ascertained by Law, and paid out of the Treasury of the United States. They shall in all Cases, except Treason, Felony and Breach of the Peace, be privileged from Arrest during their Attendance at the Session of their respective Houses, and in going to and returning from the same; and for any Speech or Debate in either House, they shall not be questioned in any other Place.

No Senator or Representative shall, during the Time for which he was elected, be appointed to any civil Office under the Authority of the United States, which shall have been created, or the Emoluments whereof shall have been increased during such time; and no Person holding any Office under the United States, shall be a Member of either House during his Continuance in Office.

Section. 7. All Bills for raising Revenue shall originate in the House of Representatives; but the Senate may propose or concur with Amendments as on other

THE UNITED STATES CONSTITUTION

We the People of the United States, in Order to form a more perfect Union, establish Justice, insure domestic Tranquility, provide for the common defence, promote the general Welfare, and secure the Blessings of Liberty to ourselves and our Posterity, do ordain and establish this Constitution for the United States of America.

Article I

Section 1

All legislative Powers herein granted shall be vested in a Congress of the United States, which shall consist of a Senate and House of Representatives.

Section 2

The House of Representatives shall be composed of Members chosen every second Year by the People of the several States, and the Electors in each State shall have the Qualifications requisite for Electors of the most numerous Branch of the State Legislature.

No Person shall be a Representative who shall not have attained to the Age of twenty five Years, and been seven Years a Citizen of the United States, and who shall not, when elected, be an Inhabitant of that State in which he shall be chosen.

Representatives and direct Taxes shall be apportioned among the several States which may be included within this Union, according to their respective Numbers, which shall be determined by adding to the whole Number of free Persons, including those bound to Service for a Term of Years, and excluding Indians not taxed, three fifths of all other Persons. The actual Enumeration shall be made within three Years after the first Meeting of the Congress of the United States, and within every subsequent Term of ten Years, in such

Manner as they shall by Law direct. The Number of Representatives shall not exceed one for every thirty Thousand, but each State shall have at Least one Representative; and until such enumeration shall be made, the State of New Hampshire shall be entitled to chuse three, Massachusetts eight, Rhode-Island and Providence Plantations one, Connecticut five, New-York six, New Jersey four, Pennsylvania eight, Delaware one, Maryland six, Virginia ten, North Carolina five, South Carolina five, and Georgia three.

When vacancies happen in the Representation from any State, the Executive Authority thereof shall issue Writs of Election to fill such Vacancies.

The House of Representatives shall chuse their Speaker and other Officers; and shall have the sole Power of Impeachment.

Section 3

The Senate of the United States shall be composed of two Senators from each State, chosen by the Legislature thereof for six Years; and each Senator shall have one Vote.

Immediately after they shall be assembled in Consequence of the first Election, they shall be divided as equally as may be into three Classes. The Seats of the Senators of the first Class shall be vacated at the Expiration of the second Year, of the second Class at the Expiration of the fourth Year, and of the third Class at the Expiration of the sixth Year, so that one third may be chosen every second Year; and if Vacancies happen by Resignation, or otherwise, during the Recess of the Legislature of any State, the Executive thereof may make temporary Appointments until the next Meeting of the Legislature, which shall then fill such Vacancies.

No Person shall be a Senator who shall not have attained to the Age of thirty Years, and been nine Years a Citizen of the United States, and who shall not, when elected, be an Inhabitant of that State for which he shall be chosen.

The Vice President of the United States shall be President of the Senate, but shall have no Vote, unless they be equally divided.

The Senate shall chuse their other Officers, and also a President pro tempore, in the Absence of the Vice President, or when he shall exercise the Office of President of the United States.

The Senate shall have the sole Power to try all Impeachments. When sitting for that Purpose, they shall be on Oath or Affirmation. When the President of the United States is tried, the Chief Justice shall preside: And no Person shall be convicted without the Concurrence of two thirds of the Members present.

Judgment in Cases of Impeachment shall not extend further than to removal from Office, and disqualification to hold and enjoy any Office of honor, Trust or Profit under the United States: but the Party convicted shall nevertheless be liable and subject to Indictment, Trial, Judgment and Punishment, according to Law.

Section 4

The Times, Places and Manner of holding Elections for Senators and Representatives, shall be prescribed in each State by the Legislature thereof; but the Congress may at any time by Law make or alter such Regulations, except as to the Places of chusing Senators.

The Congress shall assemble at least once in every Year, and such Meeting shall be on the first Monday in December, unless they shall by Law appoint a different Day.

Section 5

Each House shall be the Judge of the Elections, Returns and Qualifications of its own Members, and a Majority of each shall constitute a Quorum to do Business; but a smaller Number may adjourn from day to day, and may be authorized to compel the Attendance of absent Members, in such Manner, and under such Penalties as each House may provide.

Each House may determine the Rules of its Proceedings, punish its Members for disorderly Behaviour, and, with the Concurrence of two thirds, expel a Member.

Each House shall keep a Journal of its Proceedings, and from time to time publish the same, excepting such Parts as may in their Judgment require Secrecy; and the Yeas and Nays of the Members of either House on any question shall, at the Desire of one fifth of those Present, be entered on the Journal.

Neither House, during the Session of Congress, shall, without the Consent of the other, adjourn for more than three days, nor to any other Place than that in which the two Houses shall be sitting.

Section 6

The Senators and Representatives shall receive a Compensation for their Services, to be ascertained by Law, and paid out of the Treasury of the United States. They shall in all Cases, except Treason, Felony and Breach of the Peace, be privileged from Arrest during their Attendance at the Session of their respective Houses, and in going to and returning from the same; and for any Speech or Debate in either House, they shall not be questioned in any other Place.

No Senator or Representative shall, during the Time for which he was elected, be appointed to any civil Office under the Authority of the United States, which shall have been created, or the Emoluments whereof shall have been encreased during such time; and no Person holding any Office under the United States, shall be a Member of either House during his Continuance in Office.

Section 7

All Bills for raising Revenue shall originate in the House of Representatives; but the Senate may propose or concur with Amendments as on other Bills.

Every Bill which shall have passed the House of Representatives and the Senate, shall, before it become a Law, be presented to the President of the United States: If he approve he shall sign it, but if not he shall return it, with his Objections to that House in which it shall have originated, who shall enter the Objections at large on their Journal, and proceed to reconsider it. If after such Reconsideration two thirds of that House shall agree to pass the Bill, it shall be sent, together with the Objections, to the other House, by which it shall likewise be reconsidered, and if approved by two thirds of that House, it shall become a Law. But in all such Cases the Votes of both Houses shall be determined by yeas and Nays, and the Names of the Persons voting for and against the Bill shall be entered on the Journal of each House respectively. If any Bill shall not be returned by the President within ten Days (Sundays excepted) after it shall have been presented to him, the Same shall be a Law, in like Manner as if he had signed it, unless the Congress by their Adjournment prevent its Return, in which Case it shall not be a Law.

Every Order, Resolution, or Vote to which the Concurrence of the Senate and House of Representatives may be necessary (except on a question of Adjournment) shall be presented to the President of the United States; and before the Same shall take Effect, shall be approved by him, or being disapproved by him, shall be repassed by two thirds of the Senate and House of Representatives, according to the Rules and Limitations prescribed in the Case of a Bill.

Section 8

The Congress shall have Power To lay and collect Taxes, Duties, Imposts and Excises, to pay the Debts and provide for the common Defence and general Welfare of the United States; but all Duties, Imposts and Excises shall be uniform throughout the United States;

To borrow Money on the credit of the United States;

To regulate Commerce with foreign Nations, and among the several States, and with the Indian Tribes;

To establish an uniform Rule of Naturalization, and uniform Laws on the subject of Bankruptcies throughout the United States;

To coin Money, regulate the Value thereof, and of foreign Coin, and fix the Standard of Weights and Measures;

To provide for the Punishment of counterfeiting the Securities and current Coin of the United States;

To establish Post Offices and post Roads;

To promote the Progress of Science and useful Arts, by securing for limited Times to Authors and Inventors the exclusive Right to their respective Writings and Discoveries;

To constitute Tribunals inferior to the supreme Court;

To define and punish Piracies and Felonies committed on the high Seas, and Offences against the Law of Nations;

To declare War, grant Letters of Marque and Reprisal, and make Rules concerning Captures on Land and Water;

To raise and support Armies, but no Appropriation of Money to that Use shall be for a longer Term than two Years;

To provide and maintain a Navy;

To make Rules for the Government and Regulation of the land and naval Forces;

To provide for calling forth the Militia to execute the Laws of the Union, suppress Insurrections and repel Invasions;

To provide for organizing, arming, and disciplining, the Militia, and for governing such Part of them as may be employed in the Service of the United States, reserving to the States respectively, the Appointment of the Officers, and the Authority of training the Militia according to the discipline prescribed by Congress;

To exercise exclusive Legislation in all Cases whatsoever, over such District (not exceeding ten Miles square) as may, by Cession of particular States, and the Acceptance of Congress, become the Seat of the Government of the United States, and to exercise like Authority over all Places purchased by the Consent of the Legislature of the State in which the Same shall be, for the Erection of Forts, Magazines, Arsenals, dock-Yards, and other needful Buildings;—And

To make all Laws which shall be necessary and proper for carrying into Execution the foregoing Powers, and all other Powers vested by this Constitution in the Government of the United States, or in any Department or Officer thereof.

Section 9

The Migration or Importation of such Persons as any of the States now existing shall think proper to admit, shall not be prohibited by the Congress prior to the Year one thousand eight hundred and eight, but a Tax or duty may be imposed on such Importation, not exceeding ten dollars for each Person.

The Privilege of the Writ of Habeas Corpus shall not be suspended, unless when in Cases of Rebellion or Invasion the public Safety may require it.

No Bill of Attainder or ex post facto Law shall be passed.

No Capitation, or other direct, Tax shall be laid, unless in Proportion to the Census or enumeration herein before directed to be taken.

No Tax or Duty shall be laid on Articles exported from any State.

No Preference shall be given by any Regulation of Commerce or Revenue to the Ports of one State over those of another: nor shall Vessels bound to, or from, one State, be obliged to enter, clear, or pay Duties in another.

No Money shall be drawn from the Treasury, but in Consequence of Appropriations made by Law; and a regular Statement and Account of the Receipts and Expenditures of all public Money shall be published from time to time.

No Title of Nobility shall be granted by the United States: And no Person holding any Office of Profit or Trust under them, shall, without the Consent of the Congress, accept of any present, Emolument, Office, or Title, of any kind whatever, from any King, Prince, or foreign State.

Section 10

No State shall enter into any Treaty, Alliance, or Confederation; grant Letters of Marque and Reprisal; coin Money; emit Bills of Credit; make any Thing but gold and silver Coin a

Tender in Payment of Debts; pass any Bill of Attainder, ex post facto Law, or Law impairing the Obligation of Contracts; or grant any Title of Nobility.

No State shall, without the Consent of the Congress, lay any Imposts or Duties on Imports or Exports, except what may be absolutely necessary for executing its inspection Laws: and the net Produce of all Duties and Imposts, laid by any State on Imports or Exports, shall be for the Use of the Treasury of the United States; and all such Laws shall be subject to the Revision and Control of the Congress.

No State shall, without the Consent of Congress, lay any Duty of Tonnage, keep Troops, or Ships of War in time of Peace, enter into any Agreement or Compact with another State, or with a foreign Power, or engage in War, unless actually invaded, or in such imminent Danger as will not admit of delay.

Article II

Section 1

The executive Power shall be vested in a President of the United States of America. He shall hold his Office during the Term of four Years, and, together with the Vice President, chosen for the same Term, be elected, as follows

Each State shall appoint, in such Manner as the Legislature thereof may direct, a Number of Electors, equal to the whole Number of Senators and Representatives to which the State may be entitled in the Congress: but no Senator or Representative, or Person holding an Office of Trust or Profit under the United States, shall be appointed an Elector.

The Electors shall meet in their respective States, and vote by Ballot for two Persons, of whom one at least shall not be an Inhabitant of the same State with themselves. And they shall make a List of all the Persons voted for, and of the Number of Votes for each; which List they shall sign and certify, and transmit sealed to the Seat of the Government of the United States, directed to the President of the Senate. The President of the Senate shall, in the Presence of the Senate and House of Representatives, open all the Certificates, and the Votes shall then be counted. The Person having the greatest Number of Votes shall be the President, if such Number be a Majority of the whole Number of Electors appointed; and if there be more than one who have such Majority, and have an equal Number of Votes, then the House of Representatives shall immediately chuse by Ballot one of them for President; and if no Person have a Majority, then from the five highest on the List the said House shall in like Manner chuse the President. But in chusing the President, the

Votes shall be taken by States, the Representation from each State having one Vote; A quorum for this Purpose shall consist of a Member or Members from two thirds of the States, and a Majority of all the States shall be necessary to a Choice. In every Case, after the Choice of the President, the Person having the greatest Number of Votes of the Electors shall be the Vice President. But if there should remain two or more who have equal Votes, the Senate shall chuse from them by Ballot the Vice President.

The Congress may determine the Time of chusing the Electors, and the Day on which they shall give their Votes; which Day shall be the same throughout the United States.

No Person except a natural born Citizen, or a Citizen of the United States, at the time of the Adoption of this Constitution, shall be eligible to the Office of President; neither shall any Person be eligible to that Office who shall not have attained to the Age of thirty five Years, and been fourteen Years a Resident within the United States.

In Case of the Removal of the President from Office, or of his Death, Resignation, or Inability to discharge the Powers and Duties of the said Office, the Same shall devolve on the Vice President, and the Congress may by Law provide for the Case of Removal, Death, Resignation or Inability, both of the President and Vice President, declaring what Officer shall then act as President, and such Officer shall act accordingly, until the Disability be removed, or a President shall be elected.

The President shall, at stated Times, receive for his Services, a Compensation, which shall neither be encreased nor diminished during the Period for which he shall have been elected, and he shall not receive within that Period any other Emolument from the United States, or any of them.

Before he enter on the Execution of his Office, he shall take the following Oath or Affirmation:—"I do solemnly swear (or affirm) that I will faithfully execute the Office of President of the United States, and will to the best of my Ability, preserve, protect and defend the Constitution of the United States."

Section 2

The President shall be Commander in Chief of the Army and Navy of the United States, and of the Militia of the several States, when called into the actual Service of the United States; he may require the Opinion, in writing, of the principal Officer in each of the executive Departments, upon any Subject relating to the Duties of their respective Offices, and he shall have Power to grant Reprieves and Pardons for Offences against the United States, except in Cases of Impeachment.

He shall have Power, by and with the Advice and Consent of the Senate, to make Treaties, provided two thirds of the Senators present concur; and he shall nominate, and by and with the Advice and Consent of the Senate, shall appoint Ambassadors, other public Ministers and Consuls, Judges of the supreme Court, and all other Officers of the United States, whose Appointments are not herein otherwise provided for, and which shall be established by Law: but the Congress may by Law vest the Appointment of such inferior Officers, as they think proper, in the President alone, in the Courts of Law, or in the Heads of Departments.

The President shall have Power to fill up all Vacancies that may happen during the Recess of the Senate, by granting Commissions which shall expire at the End of their next Session.

Section 3

He shall from time to time give to the Congress Information of the State of the Union, and recommend to their Consideration such Measures as he shall judge necessary and expedient; he may, on extraordinary Occasions, convene both Houses, or either of them, and in Case of Disagreement between them, with Respect to the Time of Adjournment, he may adjourn them to such Time as he shall think proper; he shall receive Ambassadors and other public Ministers; he shall take Care that the Laws be faithfully executed, and shall Commission all the Officers of the United States.

Section 4

The President, Vice President and all civil Officers of the United States, shall be removed from Office on Impeachment for, and Conviction of, Treason, Bribery, or other high Crimes and Misdemeanors.

Article III

Section 1

The judicial Power of the United States shall be vested in one supreme Court, and in such inferior Courts as the Congress may from time to time ordain and establish. The Judges, both of the supreme and inferior Courts, shall hold their Offices during good Behaviour, and shall, at stated Times, receive for their Services, a Compensation, which shall not be diminished during their Continuance in Office.

Section 2

The judicial Power shall extend to all Cases, in Law and Equity, arising under this Constitution, the Laws of the United States, and Treaties made, or which shall be made, under their Authority;—to all Cases affecting Ambassadors, other public Ministers and Consuls;—to all Cases of admiralty and maritime Jurisdiction;—to Controversies to which the United States shall be a Party;—to Controversies between two or more States;—between a State and Citizens of another State;—between Citizens of different States,—between Citizens of the same State claiming Lands under Grants of different States, and between a State, or the Citizens thereof, and foreign States, Citizens or Subjects.

In all Cases affecting Ambassadors, other public Ministers and Consuls, and those in which a State shall be Party, the supreme Court shall have original Jurisdiction. In all the other Cases before mentioned, the supreme Court shall have appellate Jurisdiction, both as to Law and Fact, with such Exceptions, and under such Regulations as the Congress shall make.

The Trial of all Crimes, except in Cases of Impeachment, shall be by Jury; and such Trial shall be held in the State where the said Crimes shall have been committed; but when not committed within any State, the Trial shall be at such Place or Places as the Congress may by Law have directed.

Section 3

Treason against the United States, shall consist only in levying War against them, or in adhering to their Enemies, giving them Aid and Comfort. No Person shall be convicted of Treason unless on the Testimony of two Witnesses to the same overt Act, or on Confession in open Court.

The Congress shall have Power to declare the Punishment of Treason, but no Attainder of Treason shall work Corruption of Blood, or Forfeiture except during the Life of the Person attainted.

Article IV

Section 1

Full Faith and Credit shall be given in each State to the public Acts, Records, and judicial Proceedings of every other State. And the Congress may by general Laws prescribe the Manner in which such Acts, Records and Proceedings shall be proved, and the Effect thereof.

Section 2

The Citizens of each State shall be entitled to all Privileges and Immunities of Citizens in the several States.

A Person charged in any State with Treason, Felony, or other Crime, who shall flee from Justice, and be found in another State, shall on Demand of the executive Authority of the State from which he fled, be delivered up, to be removed to the State having Jurisdiction of the Crime.

No Person held to Service or Labour in one State, under the Laws thereof, escaping into another, shall, in Consequence of any Law or Regulation therein, be discharged from such Service or Labour, but shall be delivered up on Claim of the Party to whom such Service or Labour may be due.

Section 3

New States may be admitted by the Congress into this Union; but no new State shall be formed or erected within the Jurisdiction of any other State; nor any State be formed by the Junction of two or more States, or Parts of States, without the Consent of the Legislatures of the States concerned as well as of the Congress.

The Congress shall have Power to dispose of and make all needful Rules and Regulations respecting the Territory or other Property belonging to the United States; and nothing in this Constitution shall be so construed as to Prejudice any Claims of the United States, or of any particular State.

Section 4

The United States shall guarantee to every State in this Union a Republican Form of Government, and shall protect each of them against Invasion; and on Application of the Legislature, or of the Executive (when the Legislature cannot be convened), against domestic Violence.

Article V

The Congress, whenever two thirds of both Houses shall deem it necessary, shall propose Amendments to this Constitution, or, on the Application of the Legislatures of two thirds of the several States, shall call a Convention for proposing Amendments, which, in either

Case, shall be valid to all Intents and Purposes, as Part of this Constitution, when ratified by the Legislatures of three fourths of the several States, or by Conventions in three fourths thereof, as the one or the other Mode of Ratification may be proposed by the Congress; Provided that no Amendment which may be made prior to the Year One thousand eight hundred and eight shall in any Manner affect the first and fourth Clauses in the Ninth Section of the first Article; and that no State, without its Consent, shall be deprived of its equal Suffrage in the Senate.

Article VI

All Debts contracted and Engagements entered into, before the Adoption of this Constitution, shall be as valid against the United States under this Constitution, as under the Confederation.

This Constitution, and the Laws of the United States which shall be made in Pursuance thereof; and all Treaties made, or which shall be made, under the Authority of the United States, shall be the supreme Law of the Land; and the Judges in every State shall be bound thereby, any Thing in the Constitution or Laws of any State to the Contrary notwithstanding.

The Senators and Representatives before mentioned, and the Members of the several State Legislatures, and all executive and judicial Officers, both of the United States and of the several States, shall be bound by Oath or Affirmation, to support this Constitution; but no religious Test shall ever be required as a Qualification to any Office or public Trust under the United States.

Article VII

The Ratification of the Conventions of nine States, shall be sufficient for the Establishment of this Constitution between the States so ratifying the Same.

The Word, "the," being interlined between the seventh and eighth Lines of the first Page, the Word "Thirty" being partly written on an Erazure in the fifteenth Line of the first Page, The Words "is tried" being interlined between the thirty second and thirty third Lines of the first Page and the Word "the" being interlined between the forty third and forty fourth Lines of the second Page

Attest William Jackson Secretary

Done in Convention by the Unanimous Consent of the States present the Seventeenth Day of September in the Year of our Lord one thousand seven hundred and Eighty seven and of the Independence of the United States of America the Twelfth In witness whereof We have hereunto subscribed our Names,

G°. Washington
Presidt and deputy from Virginia

DELAWARE
Geo: Read
Gunning Bedford jun
John Dickinson
Richard Bassett
Jaco: Broom

MARYLAND
James McHenry
Dan of St Thos. Jenifer
Danl. Carroll

VIRGINIA
John Blair
James Madison Jr.

NORTH CAROLINA
Wm. Blount
Richd. Dobbs Spaight
Hu Williamson

SOUTH CAROLINA
J. Rutledge
Charles Cotesworth
    Pinckney
Charles Pinckney
Pierce Butler

GEORGIA
William Few
Abr Baldwin

NEW HAMPSHIRE
John Langdon
Nicholas Gilman

MASSACHUSETTS
Nathaniel Gorham
Rufus King

CONNECTICUT
Wm. Saml. Johnson
Roger Sherman

NEW YORK
Alexander Hamilton

NEW JERSEY
Wil: Livingston
David Brearley
Wm. Paterson
Jona: Dayton

PENNSYLVANIA
B Franklin
Thomas Mifflin
Robt. Morris
Geo. Clymer
Thos. FitzSimons
Jared Ingersoll
James Wilson
Gouv Morris

BIBLIOGRAPHY

Barry, Richard. *Mr. Rutledge of South Carolina*. New York: Duell, Sloan and Pearce, 1942.

Bell, Malcolm Jr. *Major Butler's Legacy*. Athens: University of Georgia Press, 1987.

Berkin, Carol. *A Brilliant Solution: Inventing the American Constitution*. New York: Harcourt, 2002.

Block, Seymour Stanton. *Benjamin Franklin: His Wit, Wisdom, and Women*. New York: Hastings House, 1975.

Boutell, Lewis Henry. *The Life of Roger Sherman*. Chicago: McClurg, 1896.

Donovan, Frank. *Mr. Madison's Constitution*. New York: Dodd, Mead, 1965.

Ernst, Robert. *Rufus King: American Federalist*. Chapel Hill: University of North Carolina Press, 1968.

Ferling, John E. *The First of Men: A Life of George Washington*. Knoxville: University of Tennessee Press, 1988.

Flower, Milton E. *John Dickinson: Conservative Revolutionary*. Charlottesville: University Press of Virginia, 1983.

Garraty, John A., and Mark C. Carnes, eds. *American National Biography*. New York: Oxford University Press, 1999.

Geiger, Sister Mary Virginia. *Daniel Carroll: A Framer of the Constitution*. PhD diss., Catholic University of America, 1943.

Grundfest, Jerry. *George Clymer: Philadelphia Revolutionary, 1739–1813*. New York: Arno Press, 1982.

Haw, James. *John and Edward Rutledge of South Carolina*. Athens: University of Georgia Press, 1997.

Jackson, Donald, and Dorothy Twohig, eds. *The Diaries of George Washington*. Vol. 5. Charlottesville: University Press of Virginia, 1979.

Klein, Milton M. *The American Whig: William Livingston of New York*. New York: Garland, 1990.

Malone, Dumas, ed. *Dictionary of American Biography*. New York: Scribner, 1961.

Masterson, William H. *William Blount*. 1954. Reprint, New York: Greenwood Press, 1969 [reprint of 1954 edition].

McCaughey, Elizabeth P. *From Loyalist to Founding Father: The Political Odyssey of William Samuel Johnson*. New York: Columbia University Press, 1980.

McLaughlin, Andrew Cunningham. *The Confederation and the Constitution: 1783–1789*. New York: Harper & Row, 1905.

Morris, Richard B. *The Framing of the Federal Constitution*. Washington, DC: National Park Service, 1986.

National Cyclopaedia of American Biography. New York: James T. White & Company, 1894.

Oberholtzer, Ellis Paxson. *Robert Morris: Patriot and Financier*. New York: Macmillan, 1903.

O'Connor, John E. *William Paterson: Lawyer and Statesman, 1745–1806*. New Brunswick, NJ: Rutgers University Press, 1979.

Randall, Willard Sterne. *Alexander Hamilton: A Life*. New York: HarperCollins, 2003.

Rossman, Kenneth R. *Thomas Mifflin and the Politics of the American Revolution*. Chapel Hill: University of North Carolina Press, 1952.

Rutland, Robert A. *James Madison: The Founding Father*. New York: Macmillan, 1987.

Smith, Charles Page. *James Wilson: Founding Father, 1742–1798*. Chapel Hill: University of North Carolina Press, 1956.

Steiner, Bernard C. *The Life and Correspondence of James McHenry*. Cleveland: Burrows Brothers, 1907.

Swiggett, Howard. *The Extraordinary Mr. Morris*. Garden City, NY: Doubleday, 1952.

Whitney, David C. *Founders of Freedom in America: Lives of the Men Who Signed the Constitution of the United States*. Chicago: Ferguson, 1965.

Williams, Frances Leigh. *A Founding Family: The Pinckneys of South Carolina*. New York: Harcourt Brace Jovanovich, 1978.

Williams, Selma R. *Fifty-Five Fathers: The Story of the Constitutional Convention*. New York: Dodd, Mead, 1970.

Wright, Esmond. *Franklin of Philadelphia*. Cambridge, MA: Harvard University Press, 1986.

Young, Eleanor. *Forgotten Patriot: Robert Morris*. New York: Macmillan, 1950.

Zahniser, Marvin R. *Charles Cotesworth Pinckney: Founding Father*. Chapel Hill: University of North Carolina Press, 1967.

INDEX